The shortest route to the East from Europe went by the North Pole, but it was impassable. At least this proved the case in 1596, when Dutch navigator William Barents made his third attempt to find the passage.

The voyage started promisingly: the wind was favorable and food supplies abundant in the waters around Bear Island.

But winter struck early, and Barents' ship soon became trapped by ice. The frozen sea left him no choice but to winter ashore.

Although it was only the beginning of September, storm followed storm in quick succession. Defying the icy winds, the sailors built a house for the winter

There were many bears, and the men used their fat as fuel for lamps and their skins to make clothes. Removing material from the boat, which was slowly breaking to pieces in the ice, they managed to construct a Dutch interior.

When spring came at the end of May, the men fashioned large boats from the broken remains of their vessel, and then they set sail for Europe. But for Barents it was too late. He died on the way, somewhere on the shores of Novaya Zemlya, an island in the Arctic Ocean

CONTENTS

NORTH POLE, SOUTH POLE
JOURNEYS TO
THE ENDS OF THE EARTH

Bertrand Imbert

DISCOVERIES

HARRY N. ABRAMS, INC., PUBLISHERS

NEW YORK

What was known of the ends of the earth in ancient times? The center of civilization was then the Mediterranean. There was contact with the East, but only philosophers gave any thought to the world beyond. A southern hemisphere was envisaged by the Greeks: Plato and Pythagoras believed there must be land on the other side of the known world, a counterbalance that stopped it from overturning. They called it Antichthon.

CHAPTER I
THE ENDS OF THE EARTH

This map of the world by Richard of Haldingham shows the state of cartography around 1300.

It was peopled by the hypothetical Antipodes—literally people "with the feet opposite" in Greek—and this fantastical universe was surrounded by a torrid zone of boiling seas, guarded by terrifying monsters.

In the 15th Century Humanists Renewed Speculation About Unknown Lands

Thus it was that in 1475 Ptolemy's *Geography* was printed. This Greek from Alexandria had drawn up charts of the earth and sky in the 2nd century A.D. They featured an Indian Ocean bordered at a latitude

"Here there is a mighty battle between learning on one side and the common herd on the other: the theory being that human beings are distributed all around the earth and stand with their feet pointing towards each other...."

Pliny the Elder
Natural History

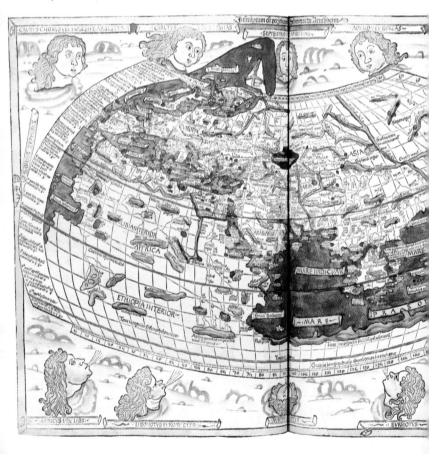

of some 20°S by a terra incognita. Many editions of the atlas were printed up to the end of the 16th century, and its ideas were widely shared by Renaissance scholars. (A plate is reproduced below.)

This was nevertheless the beginning of the age of navigational discovery. Vasco da Gama rounded the Cape of Good Hope in 1497 and sailed to India, proving that the Indian Ocean was not an enclosed sea. He had been preceded by a Chinese expedition of at least sixty-two ships under the command of Admiral Cheng Ho.

In 1520 Magellan sailed the coast of South America in search of a passage to the west. At 52°S he discovered the Strait of Magellan, which links the Atlantic to the Pacific. He believed he had found the northern shore of the Antarctic continent and called the place "Land of Fire" (Tierra del Fuego).

The first modern atlases date from 1570. That of the Flemish geographer Ortelius incorporated these discoveries, but the southern landmass was still very imprecisely described: one great continental block represented what we now know to be Tierra del Fuego, Australia, New Zealand, and the Antarctic.

Dutch Navigators Demolished the Myth of a Vast Antarctic Continent

In 1616 Le Maire and Schouten rounded Cape Horn and found that Tierra del Fuego was an island.

Twenty-five years later Abel Tasman sailed around Australia without seeing it. However, he discovered Tasmania and then the west coast of New Zealand, which he took to be the far shore of the southern continent.

Public interest in these desolate

The Portuguese navigators, being practical men, were unconcerned about the Antipodes: their primary aim was to discover the route to the southern hemisphere. They found no torrid zones or boiling seas, but green vegetation and new peoples. Ptolemy had erred about the inhabitants of the other side of the world, and the wisdom of the ancients began to be cast in doubt. After Bartholomew Diaz rounded the south end of Africa in 1488, Vasco da Gama (1469–1524, above) sailed past the Cape of Good Hope and opened the passage to India.

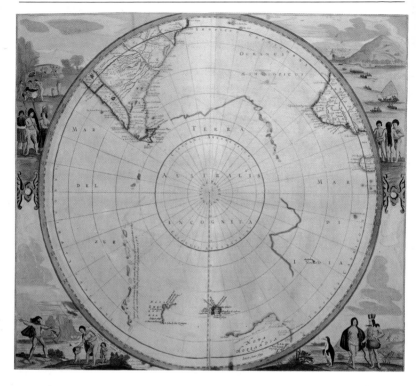

regions was, however, scant: the West was more excited by the riches of the Asian markets, and exploration of the far south was temporarily abandoned.

During the Same Period Other Navigators Ventured North

European monarchs had long dreamed of finding another route to China, via the north. There were two possibilities: the Northwest Passage, following the coast of North America, and the Northeast Passage, along the Siberian coast. A succession of expeditions ventured forth in both directions.

The French king Francis I took into his service the Florentine navigator Giovanni da Verrazano and sent

These are 17th-century maps of the Antarctic (above) and the Arctic (opposite). The word "Arctic" derives from the Greek *arktos,* meaning "bear" and referring to the constellation of the Bear, hence northern. The Greeks used the word *antarktos* to refer to the lands of the opposite pole.

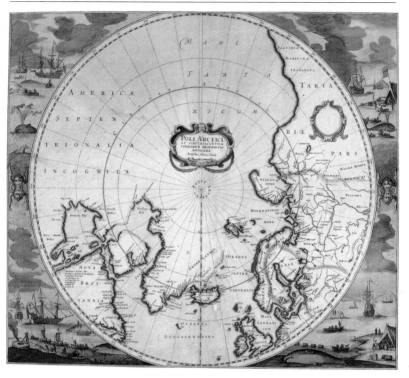

him north to look for the route to China beyond the regions reached by Christopher Columbus. In 1524 Verrazano dropped anchor in a bay that he took to be the entrance to the longed-for passage. It was in fact the mouth of the Hudson River, future site of New York City.

Ten years later Jacques Cartier discovered the St. Lawrence estuary and the following year, 1535, sailed about 600 miles upriver until he reached an Indian settlement, to which he gave the name Mont-Réal (Montreal).

The English, at the instigation of Queen Elizabeth I, penetrated much further north. From 1576 to 1578 Martin Frobisher sailed at

Jacques Cartier (1491–1557), the French sailor and explorer (below).

latitude 60°N along what was later named the Hudson Strait (Canada).

In 1585 merchants from Exeter and London financed a new expedition to China led by John Davis, a remarkable navigator and hydrographer who invented the quadrant—predecessor of the sextant—by which latitude could be precisely measured.

In the course of three expeditions Davis charted the great arm of the sea between the west coast of Greenland and the Canadian archipelago, up to latitude 72°N. Unfortunately, he reached this latitude at the end of June, too early for passage, and was stopped by the ice pack to both the north and west.

The Odyssey of the Englishman Henry Hudson

Financed by the Dutch, Henry Hudson set sail from Amsterdam in 1609 and followed in Verrazano's wake. He explored the river that now bears his name, as well as the surrounding area. Part of that area, Manhattan Island, would be named New Amsterdam when the Dutch bought it from the Indians.

In 1610 Hudson set sail again on the *Discovery*, this time backed by the English. On board were twenty-two sailors, among them his son John, age sixteen. The object of the voyage was to sail up the strait Davis had discovered.

He reached it in early August and entered a

Martin Frobisher (opposite), English adventurer and pirate, had long experience of roaming the seas when he set out in June 1576 to find the Northwest Passage to Cathay. On his voyage he met Eskimos paddling in small sealskin kayaks which excited the curiosity of the crew. Relations with the Eskimos quickly became hostile. Frobisher brought back to England an Eskimo prisoner, who caused a great stir.

vast inlet, now called Hudson Bay. Heading south, he covered some 700 miles but stayed too late and was forced to winter amid the ice.

The following spring a mutiny broke out. The rebels set him adrift in a small boat with his son and seven loyal sailors and then sailed back to England on the *Discovery*. The leaders of the mutiny died on the return trip, and the survivors were not brought to justice.

William Baffin Declared That There Was No Northwest Passage

Baffin, one of the best navigators of the age, undertook two expeditions, in 1615 and 1616. He first explored the north coast of Greenland up to latitude 78°N and then he ventured along the coast of the Canadian archipelago. Eventually he came upon Lancaster Sound, the entrance to the Northwest Passage, but, convinced it was no more than a bay, explored it no further.

On his return to England he confidently declared that no passage existed. Busy exploiting their colonies in Canada and America, the French and English gradually lost interest in the northwest route. The search did not start again for two hundred years.

An Alternative Sea Route Linked the White Sea to the Bering Strait Along Northern Siberia

This route was of great interest to England and Holland, the two great naval powers of the North Sea, who were eager to challenge Spain and Portugal's monopoly of the route to India without engaging in open conflict. The fact that geographers of the time believed the Northeast Passage to be half the length of the southern route made it the more attractive.

Contemporary atlases, such as Gerardus Mercator's, then featured a Siberia much reduced in size: it curved southeast after the Taymyr peninsula, then ran sharply south, cutting the actual route to China exactly in half. As the difficulties of navigation through ice were also underestimated, numerous explorers were drawn to the quest.

After seven winter months trapped in the ice, the *Discovery* was finally freed. By then relations between Captain Hudson and his crew had become extremely tense. Food being rationed, Hudson had favored some, while suspecting others of concealing supplies. Tactlessness compounded by misunderstanding led to mutiny, and on 23 June 1611 rebellion broke out: Hudson and eight loyal supporters were tied up and set adrift in a boat with only a small sack of meat as provisions. Meanwhile, the mutineers sailed away in the *Discovery*. On the right is John Collier's painting *The Last Voyage of Henry Hudson*.

Instead of the Northeast Passage the English Found an Ally: Ivan the Terrible

In 1553 Sir Hugh Willoughby set sail for the northeast in command of a fleet of three ships. They were to meet near the island of Vardo, off the north coast of Scandinavia.

Two of the ships, the *Bona Esperanza* and the *Bona Confidentia*, never arrived. Losing their way, they stopped for the winter on the north shore of the Kola peninsula, where all the men died, probably from carbon monoxide poisoning caused by their stove.

The third ship, the *Edward Bonaventure*, having waited for a long time at the meeting point, managed to reach Colmagro, now known as Arkhangel'sk. Chancellor, the commander, journeyed overland to Moscow, 600 miles south, to meet Ivan the Terrible.

The two men drew up a treaty that gave freedom of trade to English ships and led to the founding of the Muscovy Company. While this was beneficial to commerce, it did nothing to further the discovery of the passage.

The Dutch Navigator William Barents Was the First European to Sail East of Novaya Zemlya

Financed by the towns of Middelburg, Enkhuizen, and Amsterdam, Barents' first expedition set out in June 1594 with several ships. Barents himself, aboard the *Messenger*, headed for the north island of Novaya Zemlya, while the *Swan* and the *Mercury* set their course for the strait nearby Vaygach Island, to the south, and penetrated the Kara Sea as far as the mouth of the Ob. Barents reached the northeast point of Novaya Zemlya and approached Cape Chelyuskin. The two parties met at Vaygach and returned to Holland, certain that they had found the passage.

The following year Barents set forth again without a qualm, and seven ships laden with merchandise for

A t the entrance to the Northeast Passage Europeans first met the Samoyeds. These nomadic tribes hunted reindeer with bows and arrows. The race is still to be found in Novaya Zemlya and west of the river Ob, numbering some 25,000.

China found their passage blocked by ice at the entrance to the Kara Sea (east of Novaya Zemlya); it is impossible to predict the state of the ice pack from one year to the next.

In May 1596, on a third expedition, Barents, who was seeking a passage further to the north, discovered Spitsbergen (Norway), landed on it, and claimed it in the name of Holland.

At the end of July he again sailed along the north coast of Novaya Zemlya and saw open water to the east, but before he was able to reach it, his ship was trapped in the ice. With the rudder torn away and the hull forced up by the pressure, he was obliged to winter ashore in a house built by the sailors.

The following June the crew abandoned ship and shelter and tried to reach the Russian coast in two improvised boats. On 20 June Barents died of exhaustion or scurvy. The survivors pressed on south and were rescued by Russian ships. It was the first time that Europeans had wintered at latitude 76°N.

Three hundred years later Carlsen, the captain of a Norwegian seal boat, put in at the port where Barents had wintered. In a ruined house he found some of Barents' possessions, preserved by a layer of ice.

Interest in finding a new sea route—northeast or northwest—began to wane with Spain and Portugal's loss of supremacy. There was now open competition along the Cape route with India, the East Indies, and China.

The account of Barents' three voyages was a bestseller at the time and was translated into three languages. Below is the title page of the English edition published in 1609. The type takes the form of the hull of a boat.

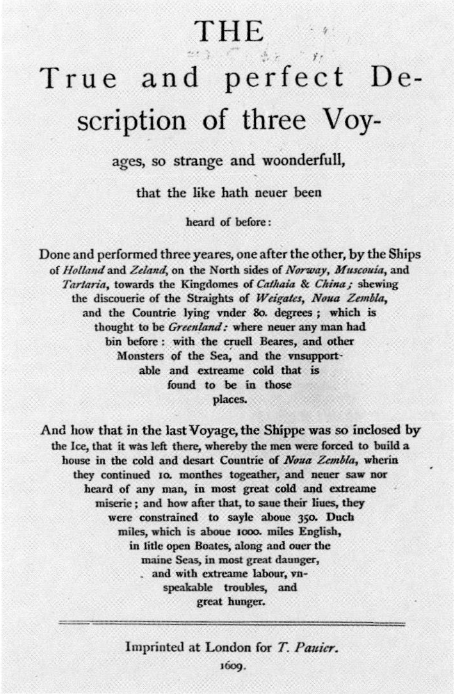

THE

True and perfect De-

scription of three Voy-

ages, so strange and woonderfull,

that the like hath neuer been

heard of before:

Done and performed three yeares, one after the other, by the Ships of *Holland* and *Zeland*, on the North sides of *Norway, Muscouia,* and *Tartaria,* towards the Kingdomes of *Cathaia* & *China*; shewing the discouerie of the Straights of *Weigates, Noua Zembla,* and the Countrie lying vnder 80. degrees ; which is thought to be *Greenland*: where neuer any man had bin before : with the cruell Beares, and other Monsters of the Sea, and the vnsupport-able and extreame cold that is found to be in those places.

And how that in the last Voyage, the Shippe was so inclosed by the Ice, that it was left there, whereby the men were forced to build a house in the cold and desart Countrie of *Noua Zembla,* wherin they continued 10. monthes togeather, and neuer saw nor heard of any man, in most great cold and extreame miserie ; and how after that, to saue their liues, they were constrained to sayle aboue 350. Duch miles, which is aboue 1000. miles English, in litle open Boates, along and ouer the maine Seas, in most great daunger, and with extreame labour, vn-speakable troubles, and great hunger.

Imprinted at London for *T. Pauier.*
1609.

This is Barents' map of the North Pole, dating from 1598. His voyages and charts of his route had an unexpected consequence: the start of whaling in the waters around Spitsbergen, where he had seen thousands of these animals. For 150 years the English and Dutch engaged profitably in whaling. Assisted by Basque harpooners, who had pioneered the whale hunt in the waters of the Bay of Biscay, they sent out up to two hundred ships. A curious discovery was made during this period: the Northeast Passage had been discovered much earlier…by whales. The whalers of Kamchatka (northeast Russia) and Japan sometimes found in their catch fragments of harpoons bearing the initials of the men who hunted the waters of Spitsbergen.

In the 17th Century Europeans Abandoned Ambitious Exploration, and the Russians Penetrated Arctic Siberia

From the early 16th century Russian navigators made the annual crossing of the Kara Sea to reach the mouth of the Ob and the Yenisey, where recent excavations have uncovered a 16th-century Siberian port, Mangazeya. They were more concerned with finding a route to China than with developing trade between Siberia and Russia. Records testify to a seaborne traffic of several thousand tons between this region and the White Sea, despite the hazards of the ice.

How can we explain the failure of the English and Dutch at a time when the Russians were using a sea route? The research of a Soviet historian of the Arctic, Mikhail I. Belov, have shown that the ships used by Barents and Chancellor were heavy and difficult to maneuver, whereas the Russians had built a fleet of boats, *kochis*, specifically adapted to the ice.

"They Were All Too Good for Us"

This was the view of Steven Borough, an English navigator who sailed the Arctic waters in 1556. In the 17th century the Russian trappers and cossacks who

A *kochi* was a 100-foot-long boat with a draft of 6.5 feet and a curved stem. A double layer of planks on the bottom and sides, up to the waterline, provided reinforcement. These features anticipated those of the first ships to navigate the passage at the end of the 19th century. With a load of forty tons, rather than the few hundred of a European ship, a *kochi* could be hauled over the ice using a winch, as in these two engravings. The size of the sails, 300 to 400 square feet, made the *kochi* much faster than European ships.

were settling in Yakutskaya in East Siberia started to use *kochis* along the Arctic coast, from the mouth of the Lena to that of the Kolyma or the Indigirka.

In 1648 a cossack, Semyon Dezhnev, took sixty hunters aboard his boats on a 1250-mile journey from the mouth of the Kolyma to the river Anadyr, famed for its fur-bearing animals. On this trip, without realizing it, he passed through the Bering Strait, the stretch of water separating Asia from America. Cape Dezhnev (just across the Bering Strait from Alaska) now bears his name.

Under Czar Peter the Great, Russia Embarked on an Extensive and Systematic Exploration of the Passage

Influenced by Leibniz and the Académie des Sciences in Paris, the czar decided in 1725, a few months before he died, to send an expedition north by sea from Kamchatka in search of a route to America. The task was entrusted to a Dane, Vitus Bering.

Bering set forth from Kamchatka in a locally built ship and reached Cape Dezhnev in mid-August 1728. Alarmed by the cruelty of the local tribes, the Chukchi, he turned back, having established that a passage existed, though he had not seen the American coast.

Now that a strait had been found between Asia and

By the mid-17th century four hundred Russian trappers had settled on the banks of the river Kolyma (eastern Russia) and were engaged in the fur trade. Some went to seek their fortune in the Far East aboard six *kochis* commanded by Dezhnev. The account of their voyage remained buried in the archives of Yakutsk until Bering's time, the following century.

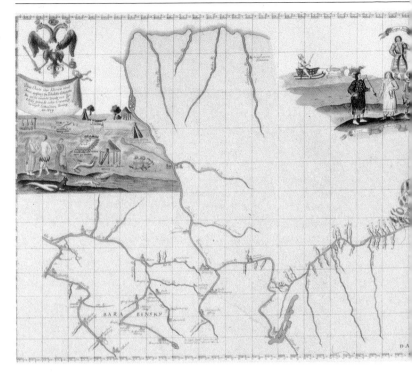

America, Empress Catherine I, wife of Peter the
Great, ordered the search for a maritime passage
along the Siberian coast to begin. Later, Empress
Anna put Bering in charge of the Great Northern
Expedition, which lasted from 1733 to 1742: five
separate expeditions were organized, involving a
total of a thousand people who divided the 310-
mile coast into five sections. *Kochis* were used but
did not always succeed in crossing the ice, particularly
as the expeditions set out early in the season. In
1741 Bering sighted the coast of Alaska and sailed
along it for four days.

   The most remarkable achievement was that of two
young naval officers, the Laptev brothers. Khariton
Laptev set forth from the mouth of the Lena in

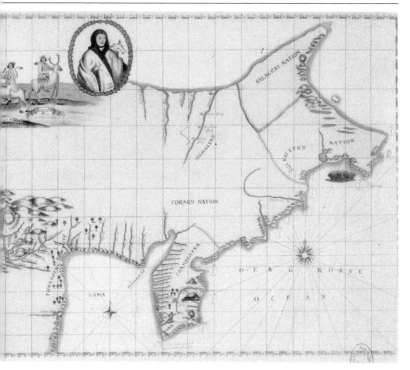

1739, made his way west, and explored the coast as far as the mouth of the Yenisey. Stopped by ice at the head of the Taymyr peninsula, he explored the region with dogsleds.

He was helped by his chief officer, Chelyuskin, who traveled overland to the northernmost point of the Asian continent, the cape that today bears his name.

Dmitry Laptev also set out from the mouth of the Lena but headed east for the Bering Strait. As he was stopped by ice, he wintered on the river Kolyma. He had managed to explore 800 miles of coast.

Fired by all these discoveries Russian merchants founded the Russian-American Company, which administered Alaska until its sale to the United States in 1867.

Bering, a Danish navigator, entered the navy of Peter the Great (left) and undertook two expeditions on which he discovered a number of the Aleutian Islands and the south coast of Alaska. The map above charts his travels from 1725 to 1730. He died in 1741 on Bering Island, returning from his second voyage.

The southern continent—which no navigator had yet located but which everyone longed to be the first to discover—was envisaged in the 18th century as a new Garden of Eden, a fertile region with a tropical climate inhabited by happy people who did not work. Philosophers dreamed that these unexplored lands would prove a rich ground for study. They hoped to find noble savages to confirm their theories.

CHAPTER II
VOYAGES TO THE FAR SOUTH

The mythical Antarctic became reality thanks to explorers such as Sir James Clark Ross (right) and Jules Dumont d'Urville, whose ship, headed for Terre Adélie, is shown trapped in the ice in the painting at left.

"I would prefer an hour of conversation with a native of the *terra australis incognita* to one with the most learned man in Europe." This was the opinion of Pierre Louis Moreau de Maupertius, French mathematician, friend of Frederick II, king of Prussia.

It Was in Search of Such a Utopia That James Cook Set Forth

Having taken advice from the astronomer Alexander Dalrymple, Cook set out in 1768. The voyage lasted until 1771. The *Endeavour*, with eighty-five men aboard, sailed past Cape Horn, Tahiti, and New Zealand. Cook's secret mission was to search for the southern continent beyond Tahiti, and on his return he declared that his voyage "must be allowed to have set aside most, if not all, the arguments and proofs that have been advanced by different authors to prove that there must be a southern continent—I mean to the northward of 40° south."

At Dalrymple's insistence the Admiralty ordered a second expedition, this time with two ships, the *Resolution* and the *Adventure*. Intended to resolve the question of the southern continent for once and for all, it lasted from 1772 to 1775. Success came on 17 January 1773: the Antarctic Circle was crossed for the first time. On his return to England Cook announced that he had circumnavigated the southern hemisphere and was "now well satisfied no continent was to be found in this ocean but must lie so far south as to be wholly inaccessible on account of ice."

Ideas about the South Pole changed: no longer was the aim to establish profitable trade with a vast southern continent, so vividly imagined by some, nor to discover the new society of which philosophers dreamed. Instead, Cook's reports of the riches of the Antarctic waters brought droves of English and American whaling boats south of Cape Horn. Based on South Georgia Island (800 miles east of the Falkland Islands), the hunters killed thousands of seals and penguins in

the space of a few years, while contributing nothing to geographical knowledge. They wished to keep their hunting grounds secret and in any case lacked the expertise to produce precise charts.

In 1819 Czar Alexander I Sent Out an Antarctic Expedition Commanded by Bellingshausen

This second voyage circumnavigating the Antarctic brought Fabian Bellingshausen within about 30 miles of the coast at latitude 69°25'S. He was probably the first man to set eyes on the continent, early in February 1820. He continued sailing east and south in the polar circle, through regions undiscovered by Cook, took shelter in Sydney in April, and set out again in November. He discovered two new territories, which he named after Peter the Great and Alexander I: Peter

The *Resolution* and the *Adventure*, with which Cook explored the South Seas, reached a latitude of 67°S in 1773. This painting shows the sailors amid the icebergs, hunting elephant seals from canoes.

Bellingshausen (left) admired Cook and ventured to the far south to complete his explorations.

Island and Alexander Island. In August 1821 he returned to Kronsthadt (Russia), after an absence of two years.

An English Firm of Shipowners Also Made Important Discoveries

Enderby Brothers, a whaling and sealing firm, put much effort into geographical discovery, in marked contrast to its competitors, and won fame thanks to two of its captains, John Biscoe and John Balleny.

John Biscoe set sail for the south in 1830 and in January 1831 sighted land south of Africa, which he named Enderby Land. He put into port at Hobart, crossed the Pacific, and discovered Adelaide Island and Graham Land south of Cape Horn.

On 9 February 1839 John Balleny, with the *Eliza Scott* and the *Sabrina*, sighted a group of islands to which he gave his name, some 550 miles east of what came to be called Terre Adélie. Then in March he discovered the Sabrina Coast to the west.

Between 1838 and 1843 American, French, and English Expeditions Ventured Towards the South Magnetic Pole, and Each Discovered a Section of the Coast

Jules Dumont d'Urville, a French naval officer famous for bringing the Venus de Milo from Greece, had already accomplished two voyages around the world when he proposed a new Pacific expedition to King Louis Philippe's minister for the navy in 1837. The Americans

In the southern ocean ships cross a zone of continual tempest, a danger to crew and vessel alike. Left: Dumont d'Urville's *Astrolabe* and *Zélée* braving the seas on 27 January 1838.

"In the afternoon, the force of the wind increased, and it blew for a gale in violent bursts, the sea very rough and the fog so persistently thick that we could see no sign of land, notwith-standing its proximity."
Journal of
Jules Dumont d'Urville

and the English seemed dangerously close to the great Pole: James Weddell had reached 74°15'S. The expedition was approved, subject to the French king's stipulation that the Antarctic waters be explored. Bonuses were offered to the crew: 100 francs for making it to latitude 75°S, and 20 francs for each additional degree.

The *Astrolabe* and the *Zélée* followed Weddell's route, but reached only 63°23'. Dumont d'Urville meanwhile charted the islands and the north shore of Graham Land (on the Antarctic Peninsula). In December 1839 the two ships put into Hobart (Tasmania, Australia) harbor: "My plan to thrust a new spearhead southwards, on the meridian of Hobart-town, was originally intended as no more than an honorable postscript to the task already achieved; but what I have learned here proves to me that this attempt amounts virtually to an obligation. The American expedition at this moment in Sydney and the expedition of James Ross, which is ever on the point of reaching here, have the same object!"

Then on 19 January 1840 Dumont d'Urville sighted the coast of the Antarctic continent. He called it Terre

"At the sight of the rocks no one on board had the slightest doubt as to the nature of the high and mighty barrier that blocked the passage of our ships. I announced to the assembled officers in the presence of the crew that this land would from henceforth bear the name Terre Adélie."
Jules Dumont d'Urville

The French flag was raised on Terre Adélie (above), while officers took measurements showing that the two ships were the first to approach the South Magnetic Pole.

Adélie after his wife Adèle. Two days later a few officers landed on a little island. The *Astrolabe* and the *Zélée* continued on their westward route, skirting the ice pack. On 29 January they sighted a ship rapidly gaining on them: it was the *Porpoise*, a brig from the expedition led by the American Charles Wilkes. Dumont d'Urville hoisted his sails, intending to join the vessel, but the young lieutenant commanding the *Porpoise* interpreted his action as a sign of flight. The two commanders went their different ways, enraged by the imagined insult.

It was not on land but on an iceberg that the crew of Wilkes' ship, the *Vincennes*, disembarked. While replenishing their water supplies, the men amused themselves by sliding on the ice.

The Wilkes Expedition Had a Commercial Purpose

In Washington in 1836, Congress and the Navy objected to southern exploration in principle. However, under pressure from President John Quincy Adams and the powerful American whaling industry, Congress yielded, and an expedition was approved.

In August 1838 an armada of six ships set sail with eighty-two officers, nine civilian naturalists, and 342 sailors on board, under the command of Lieutenant Charles Wilkes.

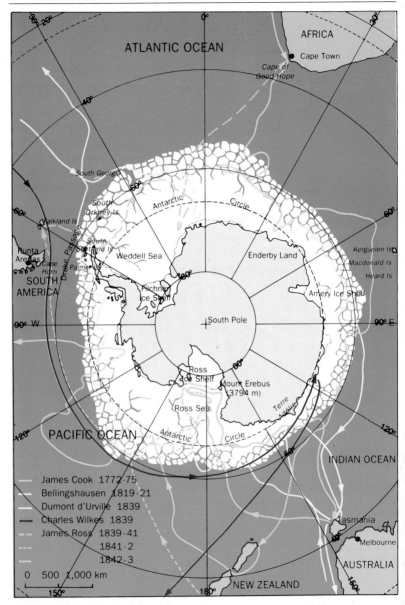

ATLANTIC OCEAN

AFRICA
● Cape Town

Cape of
Good Hope

South Georgia

South
Orkney Is

Antarctic
Circle

Falkland Is

South
Shetland Is

Weddell Sea

Enderby Land

Kerguelen Is

Macdonald Is

Heard Is

Punta
Arenas

Cape
Horn

Palmer Is

SOUTH
AMERICA

Filchner
Ice Shelf

Amery Ice Shelf

90° W

South Pole

90° E

Ross
Ice Shelf

Mount Erebus
(3794 m)

Ross Sea

Terre
Adélie

PACIFIC OCEAN

Antarctic
Circle

INDIAN OCEAN

James Cook 1772-75
Bellingshausen 1819-21
Dumont d'Urville 1839
Charles Wilkes 1839
James Ross 1839-41
        1841-2
        1842-3

Tasmania

● Melbourne

AUSTRALIA

0   500 1,000 km

NEW ZEALAND

The first expedition around Graham Land ended in failure. Two utterly inadequate vessels were sent back home, while the remainder crossed the Pacific and sought harbor in Sydney. On 26 December 1839, five days before Dumont d'Urville, Wilkes set sail for the south. On 19 January 1840, the day on which Dumont d'Urville discovered Terre Adélie, Wilkes was some 550 miles to the east. Wilkes fared better west of Terre Adélie, where he sailed along previously undiscovered coast for twelve days.

The Expedition of Sir James Clark Ross Was the Most Successful of the 19th Century

Its principal purpose was scientific: to study terrestrial magnetism. The German mathematician and astronomer Karl Friedrich Gauss had recently published a formula by which to calculate the magnetism of all parts of the earth, and the German geographer Alexander von Humboldt had proposed that it be tested.

Ross, the expedition leader, had previously located the North Magnetic Pole. At his disposal were two ships, the *Erebus* and the *Terror*, bark-rigged and reinforced for navigation through ice. The only civilian on board was Joseph Hooker, a twenty-one-year-old naturalist who was to study the lichens of the Antarctic.

The autumn of 1840 in the southern hemisphere found Ross in Hobart. The governor there, John Franklin, was a great Arctic explorer, so Ross learned about the discovery of Terre Adélie and the route taken by Charles Wilkes, which influenced his own course of action: "I therefore resolved at once to avoid all interference with their discoveries, and selected a much more easterly meridian (170°E) on which to endeavor to penetrate southward and if possible reach the magnetic pole." This decision led to the most remarkable discoveries of the 19th century.

Ross left Hobart in November 1840 with the *Erebus* and the *Terror*. In early January he had to make his way across the ice pack for four days before reaching open water, and then at 71°S he discovered Cape Adare. The

Wilkes (above) returned to the United States minus sixty sailors, who had deserted. His officers were discontented. He was court-martialed and eventually acquitted. It was years before his courage and achievement were recognized.

ships sailed on south along a great chain of mountains, which was Victoria Land: Weddell's record of 74°15'S was broken. On board bets were enthusiastically placed on a meeting of the two ships at latitude 80°S, but at latitude 77°10'S, at the end of January, the advance came to a halt before a bay, which Ross named McMurdo. It lay at the foot of a live volcano, Mount Erebus.

Leaving McMurdo (the site of the main U.S. base today), the *Erebus* and the *Terror* discovered a vast ice cliff 160 feet high and 500 miles long. Ross tried to stop for the winter on the return journey, but could find no secure site. He eventually set sail for Hobart on 6 April 1841. The success of the expedition left the men eager for further discovery.

The destination of the next expedition was that great ice cliff, the Ross Ice Shelf. On board ship were supplies for three years; however, the weather was worse than in the previous year, and Ross had to turn and head for the Falklands before reaching the ice shelf: winter had arrived.

He set out a third time, to pursue Weddell's route, but the two ships had only reached 71°30' by early March 1843, and it was too late in the season to go further. In September 1843 the *Erebus* and the *Terror* returned to England after an absence of four years.

This watercolor shows the *Terror* replenishing its water supplies on the expedition led by James Clark Ross.

The Royal Geographical Society's instructions were as follows: "The subject of most importance, beyond all question, to which the attention of Captain James Clark Ross and his officers can be turned—and that which must be considered as, in an emphatic manner, the great scientific object of the Expedition—is that of Terrestrial Magnetism."

After the Napoleonic Wars (1803–15) the British military turned to new fields in search of glory. The Admiralty, under the leadership of John Barrow, decided that England should actively engage in polar exploration.

CHAPTER III
THE RACE TO THE NORTH

The great Norwegian Arctic explorer Fridtjof Nansen (left) was the inspiration for much polar research. Lady Jane Franklin (right) organized four expeditions in search of her missing husband, Sir John. She thus helped to advance geographical knowledge of the Arctic.

In 1817, upon hearing that the Arctic waters were free of ice, Barrow launched two expeditions, while Parliament offered a reward of £5000 (over ten times a captain's salary) to the first ship to cross longitude 110°W north of the polar circle. In 1818 Englishman John Ross (the uncle of Antarctic explorer James Clark Ross) set out with the *Isabella* and the *Alexander* in search of the Northwest Passage. Although this attempt was unsuccessful, Ross' second-in-command, Edward Parry, was convinced that a passage existed, and on his return he won the support of Barrow, who was unwilling to accept defeat.

Exploration by Sea Was Backed Up by an Overland Expedition

Barrow put Parry in command of two ships, the *Hecla* and the *Griper*. He simultaneously dispatched John

"I assembled the officers, seamen, and marines of the *Hecla*, and announced to them officially, that their exertions had so far been crowned with success, as to entitle them to the first prize in the scale of rewards, granted by His Majesty's Order.... I also...directed a small addition to be made to the usual allowance of meat and some beer to be served, as a Sunday's dinner, on this occasion."

Edward Parry
Journal of a Voyage, 1821

Franklin, a veteran of the Battle of Trafalgar, on a land reconnaissance of the coast starting from Hudson Bay. Parry set out in May 1819 and reached Melville Island in September, crossing longitude 110°W and winning the £5000 reward. He gathered enough information to enable 600 miles of coast to be charted on his return to England.

Between 1819 and 1822 Franklin covered 5500 miles, 525 of which bordered the Arctic coast. In 1825 he set out again and crossed the meridian line 110°W heading east. Parry and Franklin's discoveries, together with the surveys up to the Boothia Peninsula carried out by the Hudson's Bay Company, were used to determine the likely course of the passage.

Franklin wanted to be first to find the passage, and in 1845 he set sail with the *Erebus* and the *Terror* and eventually left with 129 men. Not one came back alive.

Franklin's party reached the mouth of the Coppermine River (Northwest Territories, Canada) at the end of July 1821, and continued east in two canoes (above). For Parry, he relates in his diary, he had left "a post, which we erected on the 26th August at the mouth of Hood's River...with a flag upon it, and a letter at the foot of it, which may convey to him some useful information."
John Franklin
Narrative of a Journey
1823

In 1847 a Massive Rescue Operation Was Started: It Lasted for Ten Years, During Which Forty Ships Hunted for Traces of the *Erebus* and the *Terror*

Even when all hope was lost, Lady Jane Franklin persisted in her efforts to find her husband. Her powers of persuasion won the support of the Admiralty, the president of the United States, and finally the czar himself.

The years passed, with one expedition following another. No trace of the ships was found. Still unexplored were the waters separating Lancaster Sound from the American coast to the south. It was from here, finally, in 1854, that Eskimos reported the death of white men at the mouth of the Great Fish River (Back River, Northwest Territories).

Drawing on interest and donations from across England, Lady Jane dispatched the *Fox*, a 100-foot-long steam yacht commanded by a Captain McClintock, veteran of three expeditions. In the spring of 1859, in a cairn on King William Island, he found a canister holding messages from members of Franklin's expedition.

The notes left by the officers recorded the route taken by the *Erebus* and the *Terror* between 1845 and 1848 and the circumstances of the crew's deaths: Sir John Franklin died on 11 June 1847; the ships were abandoned on 22 April 1848; and the survivors, 105 in number, headed south on foot towards the mouth of the Great Fish River. Skeletons were later discovered, but no trace was ever found of the two ships.

A monument to Sir John Franklin and those who died with him in the quest for the Northwest Passage

The British Admiralty offered a £20,000 reward for news of Franklin's expedition. The HMS *Investigator* (left) set sail on 10 January 1850 under the command of Robert McClure in search of both Franklin's party and the Northwest Passage. For three years it was trapped by ice and did not return to England until 1853.

Sir John Franklin first set out for the Arctic in 1819. He returned in 1845, still in search of the Northwest Passage, and died in 1847 at the age of sixty-one.

After a ten-year search Franklin's death was finally confirmed. According to the papers recovered by Captain McClintock, Franklin spent the winter of 1845–6 on Beechey Island, having vainly searched for the Northwest Passage along the Wellington Channel. In the summer of 1846 the *Erebus* and the *Terror*, heading south, were trapped by ice about 12 miles northwest of King William Island. The two crews remained on board for eighteen months, then abandoned ship. None survived the march on foot. The tragedy has been dramatically rendered by artists, as in this late-19th-century painting by W. Thomas Smith, *They Forged the Last Link with Their Lives.*

The Eddystone Lighthouse, English Channel

The Quest for Franklin

Since 1845 England had not heard from Franklin. Though he had set sail on the *Erebus* and the *Terror* with provisions for at least three years, there was growing disquiet by 1847. The Admiralty consulted James Clark Ross, Edward Parry, and other experts, then decided to dispatch three expeditions along the routes Franklin was likely to have taken. The first attempts, in 1848, met with failure. New searches were organized to both west and east.

In spring 1850 a flotilla was formed under the command of Horatio Austin. It was comprised of two sailing ships, the *Resolute* and the *Assistance*, and two steamers, the *Intrepid* and the *Pioneer*, a 430-ton ship commanded by the twenty-eight-year-old Sherard Osborn. It was the first time steamers were used in ice.

The *Assistance* and the *Pioneer* in a Storm

The mission: to explore the region between the Wellington Channel and Melville Island. Private individuals also equipped and sent out ships to look for Franklin: that same year, 1850, twelve of them took to the seas.

The North Cape (Norway) at Midnight

On 3 May the fleet left England and passed the Eddystone Lighthouse. It ran into storms, icebergs, and ice cliffs.

The *Assistance* and the *Pioneer* in the Arctic, at Mount Barrow

During the summer the expedition found Franklin's first winter quarters on Beechey Island. In October the four ships were immobilized by ice in the Barrow Strait, not far from John Ross in the *Lady Franklin*.

Surrounded by Icebergs

Victoria Harbor

Temperatures in the winter camp fell as low as −58°. Largely thanks to Osborn's efforts, daily life took shape: igloos and shelters were built, dramatic performances helped fill the days, and while some went bear hunting, the more artistic sculpted the ice.

The Barrow Strait

Winter Quarters

Officers prepared the sleds and made long reconnaissance trips prior to an overland expedition planned for the spring. In April 1851 two hundred men set out in two parties, heading south and west. They surveyed the coast and the islands, covering a total of 6800 miles without finding any trace of Franklin's ships. Then in August their ships were freed from the ice, and Austin's search party returned to England disappointed men. But the search was not to end there.

The Snow Village

Fury Beach

Night Camp

Ice Bridge

The same flotilla was again dispatched, under the command of Sir Edward Belcher on board the *Assistance*. Sherard Osborn remained in command of the *Pioneer*. Together they sailed up the Wellington Channel to the Northumberland Strait, where they wintered. From 10 April to 15 July 1852 Osborn went exploring by sled. The ships headed south but were once again stopped by ice and spent the winter of 1853 in the Wellington Channel. The season went badly. There were many disputes between the touchy and dictatorial Belcher and the other officers. The following spring Belcher ordered his men to return aboard one ship and abandon the other vessels. The second expedition had been no more successful than the first.

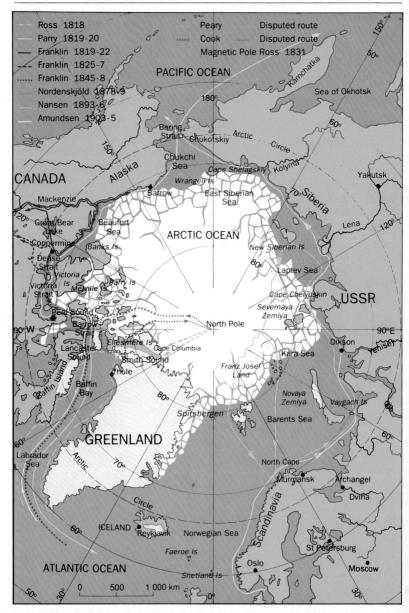

Ross 1818	Peary Disputed route
Parry 1819-20	Cook Disputed route
Franklin 1819-22	Magnetic Pole Ross 1831
Franklin 1825-7	
Franklin 1845-8	
Nordenskjöld 1878-9	
Nansen 1893-6	
Amundsen 1903-5	

now stands in Westminster Abbey, London. It was a bitter glory: for the fifty years following his death, governments and the public took little or no interest in his achievement.

In 1905 a Norwegian Discovered the Northwest Passage Virtually Singlehandedly

In 1903 aboard an old fishing boat, the *Gjoa*, loaded with provisions for three years, Roald Amundsen reached Beechey Island. He and his six companions spent two years near an Eskimo tribe, on southwest King William Island. He took measurements that enabled him to determine the position of the North Magnetic Pole and studied the Eskimo way of life and methods of surviving in the cold.

On 13 August 1905 the *Gjoa* finally set out to the west and at the end of the month met an American sailing ship from San Francisco. The Northwest Passage, occasion of so much sacrifice and heroism, had at last been found. Ironically, it was to remain largely unused.

In 1903 Amundsen spent the winter at King William Island, where half a century before, the last traces of Franklin's expedition had been found. A group of two hundred Eskimos settled near the *Gjoa*, bartering deerskin garments for needles and knives. Amundsen and his companions (below) wore native dress, which they found preferable to even the warmest European clothes.

The Northeast Passage Was Opened by the *Vega*, Which Sailed from Göteborg, Sweden, to Yokohama in Japan

On 4 July 1878 Nils Nordenskjöld left Göteborg with the *Vega* and the *Lena*. He had already undertaken expeditions to Greenland, Spitsbergen, and the Kara Sea and knew what to expect. The expedition had both scientific and commercial objectives. It was backed by the king of Sweden and two businessmen, Oscar Dickson, a Swede, and Sibiriakov, a Russian. On 19 August the two ships passed Cape Chelyuskin, at 77°34'N, a European record for eastern travel. The sea was calm, and the land stretched flat before them, lichen and moss as far as the eye could see.

Reaching the mouth of the river whose name it bore, the *Lena* sailed 930 miles upstream to Yakutsk. Meanwhile, the *Vega* pressed on to the east and, despite the ice packs, got to Cape Shelagskiy at longitude 180° by early September.

There the sea began to freeze. Though open water was only three nautical miles away and the Bering Strait but a day's sailing, Nordenskjöld had to stop for the winter. This meant nine months of waiting amid the wind and ice, bartering with the local Chukchi people.

Nordenskjöld (opposite) was forty-seven when he sailed from Sweden to Yokohama, Japan, aboard the *Vega*. This 145-foot-long whaler had a reinforced oak hull and a 60-horsepower steam engine. It was equipped with a spare rudder and propeller.

A winter evening in the officers' mess on board the *Vega*.

Lieutenant Norqvist set to work on a dictionary and grammar of the local language, while letters for Nordenskjöld's wife and the king of Sweden were entrusted to the chief of the tribe. The mail took five months to reach its destination.

On 18 July of the following year the *Vega*, freed from the ice, continued on its way and arrived in Yokohama

"June 12th [1881]....
At 1 A.M. were turned out
by ice opening in the
midst of our camp.
Transported all our gear
and belongings to a place
of safety.... At 3 A.M. the
ship had sunk until her
smoke-pipe top was
nearly awash. At 4 A.M.
the *Jeannette* went down.
First righting to an even
keel, she slowly sunk."
George W. De Long
*The Voyage of the
Jeannette,* 1884

In a message found after his death, Commander De Long related the fate of the *Jeannette.* The thirty-three crew members were left on the ice pack, with three boats, at 76°38'N and 150°30'E. On 11 July they approached a new island, Bennett Island. From there they went south and reached Semenovski Island, about 100 miles from the estuary of the Lena, on 10 September. Two days later they set sail again but were separated by a storm. Each boat met a different fate. The eleven men aboard the whaleboat were rescued by Russian outlaws living on the coast. The second boat was lost with its crew of seven. The men in the third, commanded by De Long, died of hunger and exhaustion.

on 2 September to an enthusiastic welcome. The Emperor gave Nordenskjöld an audience and decorated him for his achievement. On his return journey via the south of Asia there was celebration in every port. In Paris he was greeted by the French president and Victor Hugo, and when the *Vega* reached Stockholm on 24 April, King Oscar declared it a national holiday.

What Lay at the End of the World? An Ocean Or a Continent?

In 1879 James Gordon Bennett, the powerful owner of the New York *Herald*, famous for sending Stanley in search of Dr. Livingstone, was still on the lookout for new stories to offer his readers. Deciding to investigate the mystery of the North Pole, he sent a small steamboat, the *Jeannette*, into the ice north of the Bering Strait.

The venture was a total failure: in June 1881 at 77°15'N the *Jeannette* was smashed to pieces. Only a few survivors reached America, thanks to Russian help. Three years later, in 1884, a young Norwegian, Fridtjof Nansen, heard that Eskimos had found wreckage from the *Jeannette* on the southwest coast of Greenland, 2900 nautical miles from where the ship had foundered.

The debris, carried by the ice, had crossed the Arctic Ocean at a rate of two or three miles per day. It occurred to Nansen that the same route could be taken in a ship designed to withstand the pressure of the ice: being stuck in the ice at the Pole did not, apparently, preclude movement.

In 1890 Nansen was twenty-nine and a qualified scientist. He had just skied across Greenland and was in peak physical condition for an expedition. He approached various learned societies with his ideas.

Nansen's speculations as to whether the North Pole consisted of sea or land were received with condescension in England and skepticism in America, but with enthusiasm in Norway and Sweden. Funded by the

On reaching the mouth of the Lena, De Long sent the ship's carpenter, Nindemann, and a companion to seek help. At the end of an exhausting march they were found by natives, but all attempts to explain their situation and obtain assistance were in vain: there was no common language. The bodies of De Long and his companions were discovered several months later.

Norwegians, Nansen and a Scottish architect, Colin Archer, designed a boat named the *Fram*. Its rounded hull was intended to lift under pressure from ice.

On 24 June 1893 the *Fram* Set Out from the Port of Bergen with Twelve Men and Thirty Dogs on Board

Nansen sailed the Northeast Passage along the coast of Siberia and, as he had planned, towards the end of September reached the edge of the ice pack at 77°14'N, above the mouth of the Lena, in eastern Russia. On 24 September his diary records: "Fog in the morning, which cleared off as the day went on, when we discovered that we were closely surrounded on all sides by tolerably thick ice.... A dead region this; no life in any direction, except a single seal in the water; and on the floe beside us we can see a bear track some days old."

On board ship, protective measures were put into effect for the winter, and the rudder was lifted into a special shaft. "All at once in the afternoon as we were sitting idly chatting, a deafening noise began, and the whole ship shook. This was the first ice pressure. Everyone rushed on deck to look. The *Fram* behaved beautifully, as I had expected she would."

The first six weeks were nonetheless far from reassuring: the *Fram* drifted towards the southeast—precisely the opposite of what Nansen had intended—until December, when the direction reversed and the ship returned to the latitude it had occupied two months previously. The Arctic crossing then began.

A year later, after monotonous days enlivened by the rare sighting of a bear, the *Fram* had covered about 350 miles and was approaching the North Pole. However, the direction of the drifting was not likely to carry the vessel beyond 85°N.

The *Fram* Might Never Reach the Pole, But Nansen Was Not Giving Up

Taking a companion, three sleds, two kayaks, and twenty-seven dogs, Nansen set out first for the Pole, and afterwards for the archipelago called Franz Josef

Nansen (above) and his ship (opposite) drew many critics. Admiral Nares rejected claims that the shape of the *Fram* would cause it to rise under pressure from the ice. He considered the rounded hull to be irrelevant, claiming the ship and the ice enclosing it would form one block. Joseph Hooker, last survivor of the James Clark Ross Antarctic expedition, believed the *Fram* could resist the ice only if it scarcely projected below the waterline. And the American general Adolphus Washington Greely felt that Nansen had no experience in the Arctic and was leading his men to certain death.

The polar basin that Nansen explored in the *Fram* is an ocean many thousands of feet deep covered by sea ice 10 to 13 feet thick. Though there is no swell, the ice is in constant movement, subject to the pull of tide, wind, and ocean currents. This movement creates pressure ridges, or hummocks: the edges of two blocks, or floes, are pushed together and can form shelves as high as 13 feet with a draft of over 50 feet. It is hard to measure a ship's position when one is obliged constantly to cross or avoid these ridges, so dead reckoning is hazardous.

"The ice was here, the ice was there, The ice was all around: It cracked and growled, and roared and howled, Like noises in a swound!"
Samuel Taylor Coleridge
The Rime of the Ancient Mariner, 1798

Land, 1100 miles away. He anticipated four or five months en route during the Arctic spring.

Nansen and his companion, Frederick Johansen, carried provisions for a hundred days. According to the cruel law of the Arctic, the dogs were to be killed as needed to feed the others. It was 14 March 1895 when they left, the Pole about 400 miles distant.

By 8 April they had only reached 86°3'N: 140 miles had taken three weeks, progress being slowed by ridges of ice, or hummocks. The two men were forced to turn around and head for Franz Josef Land, about 400 miles to the south-southwest. The spring brought channels of melting water. At each one dogs and supplies had to be loaded into kayaks for the crossing.

On Wednesday 24 July Nansen recorded, "At last the marvel has come to pass—land, land.... After nearly two years, we again see something rising above that never-ending white line on the horizon yonder." It was the northeast extremity of the Franz Josef archipelago, where Nansen discovered an island, which he named Eva, after his wife. By this stage only two dogs remained alive; fortunately there were seals and bears to hunt.

On 7 August, in a channel of open water between the ice shelf and the first visible island, the men tied two kayaks together to form a catamaran and covered 100 miles under sail in three weeks, heading southwest.

Then winter came. Landing on the nearest island, the two men made ready. They killed bears and skinned them for clothing, built a stone hut, and used walrus blubber for fuel. They survived the cold season like Eskimos.

On 19 May 1896 Nansen and Johansen Set Out Again

Their destination was Spitsbergen, where they hoped

When Nansen and Johansen (below) first sighted the Franz Josef archipelago, it was summer. Many young birds were learning to fly among the yellow poppies. One evening the snow was pink: tiny algae had transformed the usual whiteness of the landscape. The bears had gone; instead, the men had to beware of walruses, liable to attack the kayaks with their ivory tusks.

to find a Norwegian seal boat to take them home. However, they were no longer very sure of their bearings and, forced to stop by frequent snowstorms, took three weeks to reach open water. Tying the kayaks together again, they sailed the coast of what appeared to be Franz Josef Land.

On 17 June, on an overland reconnaissance trip, Nansen thought he heard the bark of a dog and then the voice of a man:

"Who was it?... I raised my hat; we extended a hand to one another. On one side the civilized European with an English check suit and high rubber water boots, well shaved, well groomed...on the other side the wild man, clad in dirty rags, black with oil and soot, with long, uncombed hair and shaggy beard.... Suddenly he stopped, looked me full in the face, and said quickly,

'Aren't you Nansen?'

'Yes, I am.'

'By Jove! I am glad to see you.'" The man was called Jackson.

Nansen had reached Cape Flora, an English base. On 7 August he boarded the *Windward*, a supply ship from the Jackson expedition, and eight days later he landed at Vardo, Norway.

The Race to the North Pole: Andrée Made the First Attempt in a Balloon

The quest for the geographic North Pole was not solely of scientific interest— many people were drawn to it by a taste for adventure and fame.

Salomon Andrée, a Swedish engineer, saw the balloon as the solution to the obstacles posed by streams

Nansen made it back to Vardo, Norway, but what became of the *Fram*, which had been abandoned in the ice? Nansen had left Otto Sverdrup in command on 14 March 1895. On 20 August 1896 Nansen was on board the *Otaria*, Sir George Baden Powell's yacht, when a telegram arrived: "For Fridtjof Nansen; *Fram* arrived in good condition. All well on board. Shall start at once for Tromsö [northern Norway]. Welcome home. Otto Sverdrup." No sooner had Sverdrup reached Tromsö after a three-year voyage than he hastened to the post office to obtain news of Nansen. The two men met in Tromsö on 25 August, to be welcomed as heroes.

Three days after taking off from Spitsbergen —on 14 July 1897— Andrée's balloon, the *Eagle*, was caught in the fog and weighed down by a film of ice (left). It landed on the sea ice about 350 miles northeast of Danes Island, and for two months the three men made their way on foot through decayed ice and half-melted snow. Fraenkel and Strindberg can be seen (inset top) next to a polar bear, their main source of food. They advanced only a mile or so a day, exhausted by both the physical exertion (inset bottom) and their diet. Early in October they reached White Island, a rocky islet at about 80°N on which they ended their days. Over thirty years later two sailors from a Norwegian seal boat discovered Fraenkel's body in a small boat, with the *Eagle's* log book, the two men's journals, and some exposed film.

and hummocks. At the time, 1896, hot-air balloons had been in existence for over a century, airships were imminent, airplanes but a dream.

Andrée had no difficulty persuading the king of Sweden and the philanthropist Alfred Nobel to support his first attempt on the Pole. The balloon was built in Paris and christened the *Eagle*, or *Ornen* in Swedish.

However, when they tried to take off from Spitsbergen, the chosen point of departure 1860 miles away, winds proved unfavorable. Andrée gave up the attempt and deflated his balloon.

The following year he tried again and took off on 11 July accompanied by Nils Strindberg, a photographer, and Knut Fraenkel, an engineer. They were never seen alive again.

It was thirty-three years later that the Norwegian seal boat *Bratvaag* chanced upon the men's last camp on White Island and brought back their papers, photographs, and last letters. They had died in October.

In 1899 Louis Amadeus, the Young Italian Prince of Savoy-Aosta and Duke of the Abruzzi, Set Out for the Pole

Aboard the *Stella Polare* he reached Cape Fligeli, at 81°50'N the northernmost extremity of Rudolf Island in the Franz Josef archipelago. During the winter the prince got frostbite in two fingers and was unable to lead the attempt on the Pole.

Umberto Cagni, one of his officers, set out on 13 March 1900 with thirteen sleds. Progress was hard, averaging less than six miles a day, and three men perished. On 24 April latitude 86°34'N was reached. Nansen's record was marginally beaten; but the Pole remained to be conquered.

These pictures, taken from two periodicals of the time, the *Petit Journal* and *La Domenica del Corriere*, illustrate the interest in polar expeditions in the early part of the century. With the cheer of the crowd ringing in his ears, the Duke of the Abruzzi (below), nephew to the king of Italy, left Turin station to rejoin his ship in polar waters. The rival claims of Frederick Cook and Robert Peary to have been first at the North Pole was another subject of universal interest.

Peary Versus Cook: Good News or False Claims?

In the same period Robert Peary, a civil engineer in the
U.S. Navy, also nursed the ambition to conquer the
Pole. Between 1886 and 1908, financed by a group of
American businessmen, the Peary Arctic Club,
he organized eight expeditions. The first took
place in the Canadian archipelago and
north of Greenland and gave him practical
experience. In particular, he learned
Eskimo survival techniques, which proved
useful on his 1908–9 expedition.

With his ship, the *Roosevelt,* he landed
on the northwest coast of Greenland in
August 1908 and took on board several
Eskimo families and 246 dogs. He
wintered on Cape Sheridan, preparing his
expedition in minute detail. The men
hunted polar bear, caribou, and musk ox
and built up stores of smoked meat and fat
to provide heat and light; they made sleds
and harnesses for the dogs, and the women
stitched clothing and boots.

On 1 March 1909 Peary set out from Cape
Columbia, Ellesmere Island, with 17 Eskimos,
19 sledges, 133 dogs, his longstanding servant
and companion Matthew Henson, and five other
men. After a month the last support team turned
back at latitude 87°47'N. Peary headed on north
with Henson.

On 27 April Peary returned aboard the *Roosevelt*
in triumph, claiming that on 6 April he had reached
the Pole. On his arrival at Indian Harbor on 5
September he wired his wife: "Have made good at
last. I have the Pole. Am well. Love." It was the start
of a fierce controversy.

On 1 September the New York *Herald,* always in the
lead in matters concerning the frozen North, received a
telegram from Frederick Cook claiming he had reached
the North Pole the previous year and discovered a new

land. Cook was an American doctor who had been with Peary in north Greenland.

During 1907–8, on an expedition financed by a rich American, John Bradley, Cook had wintered in Anoatak, an Eskimo village 800 miles from the Pole, well to the south of Cape Columbia. He set forth on 19 February 1908 with eleven Eskimos, eleven sleds, and 103 dogs and claimed to have reached the Pole on 21 April. Compelled to spend the winter in a cave at Cape Sparbo on the north coast of Devon Island, however, he did not return to base until 15 April 1909, after an absence of fourteen months.

On 8 September 1909 Peary, in an interview with the press, claimed that Cook "has not been at the pole on April 21st 1908 or at any other time. He has simply handed the public a gold brick." This statement was tantamount to an open declaration of war between the two former companions.

The newspapers provided sensational coverage. While the *Herald* supported Cook, the *New York Times* backed Peary, as did the powerful National Geographic Society. The affair acquired political dimensions. After an angry debate Congress voted: by 135 votes to 34, Peary was declared the official victor and given the title of Rear Admiral.

This did not end the argument, fueled as it was by the absence of proof. How could Peary have achieved a daily average of 44 miles when Nansen, Cagni, and indeed Peary himself on earlier sorties, had never exceeded 9 miles per day? And the lack of precise information

Neither Robert Peary (left) nor Frederick Cook (below) can be proven to have conquered the North Pole, since neither took observations of longitude or declination. This was not done until 23 April 1948, when four Russians landed at the Pole in three airplanes and calculated their position: 90° exactly.

concerning dates, astronomical observations, and sled loads made Cook's venture to the Pole inherently improbable—although having survived a year in the frozen north on local resources was in itself a remarkable achievement.

Amundsen, First to Navigate the Northwest Passage, First to Find the South Pole, Set Out to Fly to the Frozen North at the Age of Fifty-Two

In the autumn of 1924 Roald Amundsen was on a lecture tour in America when the telephone rang in his room at the Waldorf Astoria in New York. It was Lincoln Ellsworth, an engineer and millionaire interested in polar exploration, offering to finance Amundsen's next expedition. He was to become both a loyal friend and a fellow explorer.

The project Amundsen then had in mind was an air expedition to the North Pole with the object of exploring the region between Spitsbergen and the Pole for the first time. On his return to Norway he began his preparations. He and Riiser Larsen, a young officer in the naval air services, chose two Dornier-Wals, flying boats of Italian construction. (Flying boats are seaplanes with hulls adapted for floating.) They planned to land on the Pole, abandon one flying boat after having taken its fuel, and then fly to Alaska over little-known regions.

On 21 May 1925 six men set out: Roald Amundsen, Lincoln Ellsworth, Riiser Larsen and Leif Dietrichsen (the pilots), and two mechanics. In eight hours of flight against a strong northeast wind they consumed half their fuel and landed on a channel of open water at latitude 87°44'N, 155 miles from the Pole. One of the planes was damaged, and moving ice blocked the way. It took three weeks to make a 650-foot airstrip on a large floe. The flying boat finally took off on 14 June and eight hours later landed near North Cape. When the expedition returned to Oslo on 5 July, it was to a big welcome from the king and queen and all the ships in the harbor.

Lincoln Ellsworth (above) was forty-four years old when he met Amundsen (left) and financed his aerial expedition. The two flying boats, Dornier-Wals fitted with 360-horsepower Rolls Royce engines, were equally able to land on water or snow.

Another First: An Airship, the *Norge*, Reached the North Pole in 1926

The airplanes of the period did not have the range for long polar flights, and aerial exploration remained hazardous. An airship, however, had a considerable radius of action and could land anywhere in calm weather. In Italy Riiser Larsen had met Umberto Nobile, an engineer who was building a semirigid airship, later to be called the *Norge*.

The *Norge* left Rome on 10 April 1926 and on 7 May landed at King's Bay, Spitsbergen, to find the American expedition of Commander Richard E. Byrd and the aviator Floyd Bennett, who flew to the Pole in a three-engine Fokker the following day. Their flight there and back took 15 hours, 30 minutes, a result that was disputed on grounds of weather conditions and the speed of the plane.

The *Norge* set out on 11 May at 8:50 A.M. and took 16 hours, 40 minutes to reach the Pole. Descending to an altitude of 656 feet, the airship flew the national flags of the expedition, representing Norway, the United States, and Italy. Whereas the hydrographer Rollin Harris had envisaged a continent between the Pole and Alaska, all that the crew of the *Norge* could see was the ice pack covering what was henceforth called the Arctic Ocean.

On 14 May, after a 72-hour flight, the *Norge* finally landed in the little village of Teller, in Alaska.

Built by Umberto Nobile, the N-1 was a semirigid airship 24,800 cubic yards in volume, fitted with three Maybach engines of 250 horsepower. It had a carrying capacity of 23 tons and could fly 5000 miles, twice the distance between Spitsbergen and Nome, Alaska. Amundsen and his colleagues were determined to attempt the crossing to the Pole in Nobile's airship. The project won the approval of the Italian Prime Minister Benito Mussolini, leader of the Fascist party. Eager for both glory and publicity, he was willing to donate the N-1 on the condition that it flew the Italian flag. Instead, the Norwegians bought the airship for $75,000 and renamed it the *Norge*.

"It Would Be Better Not to Tempt Fate Twice," Mussolini Said to Nobile

Italy was enraptured by Nobile's success. Airships were now seen as the transport of the future, and there was talk of establishing a line from Rome to Rio de Janeiro. But Nobile had other ideas: to use the airship for scientific exploration in the Arctic.

Despite Mussolini's reservations, Nobile flew from Milan on 15 April 1928 on the *Italia*, companion to the *Norge*. On 6 May he reached King's Bay, where he met an Italian supply ship, the *Città di Milano*. From here he made several flights over the islands of Siberia.

The *Italia* reached the Pole on 23 May: Nobile dropped an Italian flag and a great oak cross. On the way back to Spitsbergen the airship ran into fog, ice, and opposing winds of 20 to 25 knots.

Members of the *Norge* expedition: seated, left to right: Amundsen, Ellsworth, and Nobile.

While the three men were in many ways complementary, their cultural differences were a source of conflict.

Thirty Hours after Leaving the Pole the *Italia* Was Caught in a Snowstorm. At 7:30 P.M. on 25 May the Airship Violently Struck the Ice

Nobile and eight of his companions found themselves on the ice pack. Amid the wreckage of the gondola were provisions for forty-five days, a tent, a revolver, and, miraculously, a radio that one of the crew had grabbed at the moment of impact.

The storm bore away the *Italia,* which was lost forever, with seven passengers still on board. The survivors were 60 miles north of Northeast Land, with Nobile and the mechanic wounded, which precluded setting out on foot. Nobile regularly sent out distress signals that gave his position. The *Città di Milano* had raised the alert but did not hear the SOS; nor did any of the radios in Europe that were tuned in for signals after reports of the *Italia*'s disappearance.

In the absence of a response, three men, Zappi, Mariano, and Malmgren, set out on 1 June to find help. Five days later a Russian amateur radio operator picked up the SOS, and contact was made with the *Città di Milano*.

Six countries sent rescue parties, in all eighteen ships, twenty-two planes, and 1500 men.

The Russians contributed two ice-breakers, the *Malyguin* and the *Krassin*, each carrying a Junker plane.

Amundsen heard the news in the middle of a banquet in Oslo. Asked by journalists whether he intended to take part in the rescue operations, he replied, "I am ready to leave at once." These words sealed his fate.

Despite having sought the help of Swedish and Norwegian governments, Mussolini rejected Amundsen's offer, considering him an enemy of Italy because of his disagreements with Nobile on the expedition of the *Norge*. Riiser Larsen therefore led the Norwegian rescue party, while Amundsen, who was incensed, determined to go at all costs and eventually accepted an offer from the French government of a Latham 47, ill adapted to polar flights. Piloted by Captain Guilbaud, Amundsen and four companions took off from Tromsö on 18 June. They were never seen again.

Operations aboard the *Krassin* (above) were directed by an experienced polar explorer, Professor Samoilovitch. North of Spitsbergen the ice-breaker ran into very hard ice, which damaged the rudder and broke the propeller on the port side. The icebreaker nonetheless continued on its route, guided by Nobile, who was in constant radio contact. On 11 July the *Krassin* finally moored alongside the red tent and took on board the last five survivors, Viglieri, Behounek, Trojani, Cecioni, and Biagi.

Nobile (above) was greeted by rapturous crowds on his return to Rome, but Mussolini ordered an official inquiry. Acquitted, but humiliated by spiteful criticism, he went to build airships in Russia. He died in Italy in 1978, leaving his account, *My Polar Flights*.

Thirty Days After the Accident, Help Arrived

On 24 June a Swedish single-engine aircraft landed by the red tent of the survivors of the *Italia* and took off again with one passenger: Nobile, who went at the request of the others to organize the rescue.

Einar Lundborg, the Swedish pilot, returned to collect the rest of the party but somersaulted on landing and had to join them instead. Nobile was soon criticized for being the first to leave. However, he played a crucial role in guiding the Russians.

On 10 July the plane from the icebreaker *Krassin* spotted two men making signals. They proved to be Zappi and Mariano, who had set out for help over a month earlier. Malmgren, his feet frostbitten, had chosen to die rather than delay his companions. The *Krassin* rescue party arrived three days later. Zappi was warmly dressed and remarkably fit, while his companion was thinly clad and very weak. Zappi was accused, without proof, of cannibalism.

That same evening the *Krassin* rescued the remaining five survivors in the red tent.

The "Discovery" in Winterquarters. 1903.

E.A.W.

L ondon, 1895. "The exploration of the Antarctic regions is the greatest piece of geographical exploration still to be under-taken…before the end of the century." The Sixth International Geographical Congress thus relaunched the attack on the Antarctic, strangely neglected for the previous fifty years.

CHAPTER IV

INTO THE HEART OF THE ANTARCTIC

The story of the South Pole is inseparable from the drama of Scott. In 1903 he braved the ice pack aboard the *Discovery* (opposite). Robert Falcon Scott and his companions (left) reached the Pole on 17 January 1912 to find that Amundsen had arrived there before them.

Adrien de Gerlache, a Belgian Naval Officer, Was Eager to Respond to the Call

He left Antwerp aboard the *Belgica* in August 1897. With him were Frederick Cook, the American doctor who had been in the north of Greenland with Robert Peary, and then Roald Amundsen.

During the summer, January and February 1898, they explored part of Graham Land, then headed east across the Bellingshausen Sea and were beset by ice. They spent the winter drifting at the mercy of the winds, 170 miles from the coast.

Plagued by scurvy and anemia, the men were saved by Cook's prescription of a diet of seal and penguin meat. The harsh winter yielded a mass of information on climatic conditions, which proved very useful to later expeditions.

In the early 20th century, nine countries were exploring the Antarctic, carrying on the tradition of great scientific voyages.

The Swede Otto Nordenskjöld, whose uncle had discovered the Northeast Passage, set out for the Weddell Sea. While he wintered on the east coast of Graham Land, his ship, the *Antarctic*, became trapped in the frozen sea a short distance to the north, was crushed by ice, and sank.

The Germans, previously little involved in the Poles, built a ship inspired by the *Fram*: the *Gauss*, aboard

Berlin, 29 September 1899, Seventh International Geographical Congress. Scott speaking: "In recent times much reliance has been placed upon dogs for Arctic traveling. Yet nothing has been done with them to be compared with what men have achieved without dogs. Indeed, only one journey of considerable length has ever been performed, in the Arctic regions, with dogs—that by Mr. Peary across the inland ice of Greenland. But he would have perished without the resources of the country, and all his dogs, but one, died, owing to overwork, or were killed to feed the others. It is a very cruel system." Nansen got up and answered: "I have tried with and without dogs; in Greenland I had no dogs; then in the Arctic I used dogs, and I find that with dogs it is easier.... It is cruel to take dogs; but it is also cruel to overload a human being with work."

which Eric von Drygalski sailed to Kaiser Wilhelm II Land, where he spent the winter carrying out a magnetic survey.

In England the Royal Geographical Society Gave Its Full Backing to an Expedition Continuing the Work of Sir James Clark Ross

In 1899 the Royal Geographical Society president, Sir Clements Markham, obtained the initial funds from an industrialist, Llewellyn Longstaff, and the press magnate Alfred Harmsworth, founder of the *Daily Mail.* Impressed by the German projects, the government provided the rest of the money. Markham had the *Discovery* built and recruited the crew.

The Admiralty supplied most of the officers on special assignment, notably the expedition leader Markham wanted: Commander Robert Falcon Scott, thirty-two years old and a novice to polar regions, who was to become both hero and casualty.

The team included scientists, among them the naturalist Edward Wilson, who was with Scott at the end; two officers from the merchant navy; Armitage,

Nansen recommended the use of dogs, but Scott asked his men to pull the sleds. This was more than a technical divergence between two schools of explorers: Scott was following a tradition of the Royal Navy and showing an English belief in unaided personal effort, as well an English love of animals.

a veteran of Jackson's Arctic team; and the twenty-six-year-old Ernest Shackleton, who became a great polar explorer.

Fridtjof Nansen had advised the use of sled dogs, but unfortunately neither Scott nor later Shackleton paid heed. The *Discovery* spent the winter of 1902 in McMurdo Sound at the foot of Mount Erebus. Early in November Scott, Wilson, and Shackleton set out south, pulling their sleds themselves.

At the end of December the three men turned back, tormented by hunger, Shackleton being the first to succumb to scurvy. The *Discovery* was still iced in at the end of January 1903, but a relief ship, the *Morning*, had moored 10 miles away. Scott sent

Shackleton back to England with a number of others and remained for a second winter, as Markham had secretly instructed him to do. Faced with a *fait accompli*, the Admiralty could only protest and take control of operations the following year.

After an uneventful year, two ships came from the Admiralty to rescue the explorers, and Scott was ordered to abandon the *Discovery* by 15 February. Fortunately on that very day a southeast wind arrived and dispersed the ice: the *Discovery* sailed to New Zealand.

The Expeditions of Charcot, from the *Français* to the *Pourquoi-Pas?*

The son of a well-known neurologist, Jean-Baptiste Charcot was a doctor by training and an explorer by vocation. He left Brest on 31 August 1903 aboard the *Français*, a three-masted ship wintered at Wandel Island, and carried out a hydrographic survey of 550 miles of coast. On his return to France in 1905 he was much acclaimed, and the government decided to finance his new ship, the *Pourquoi-Pas?*

Charcot set sail from Le Havre on 15 August 1908 and headed due south. He recognized Adelaide Island,

"Where does the strange attraction of the polar regions lie, so powerful, so gripping that on one's return from them one forgets all weariness of body and soul and dreams only of going back? Where does the extraordinary charm of these deserted and terrifying regions lie?"
Jean-Baptiste Charcot

Charcot took a team of naval officers and scientists with him aboard the *Français* and the *Pourquoi-Pas?* and gathered valuable scientific information. Many islands and sites still bear the French names he gave them.

escaped shipwreck on the shoals of the Faure Islands, and approached Alexander Island, which is the size of Ireland and was not explored until 1938, by John Rymill. After wintering a little to the north, on Peter-mann Island, he sailed along the ice pack up to longitude 120°W. This was Charcot's last trip to the south.

After the First World War, he concentrated his explorations on the Greenland Sea. The *Pourquoi-Pas?* sailed the waters of the Arctic for many years, until Charcot drowned on 16 September 1936, in a storm off the coast of Iceland.

Into the Heart of the Antarctic: Shackleton's Expedition

After his forced repatriation in 1903 Shackleton was eager to set out again. Convinced he could outdo Scott, he tried to raise money in London for an expedition to the geographical South Pole. An industrialist, William Beardmore, finally pledged support in February 1907, on a Friday. The following Monday Shackleton was in the office of the secretary of the Royal Geographical Society, where distinguished visitors were due that very day: Amundsen, who had come to give a talk on his voyage along the Northwest Passage, and Nansen, now Norwegian ambassador to Britain. The next day *The Times* carried a report of Amundsen's talk and announced a new British expedition to conquer the South Pole.

All was set for departure: a little seal boat, the *Nimrod*; the team of sixteen, including three geologists, Thomas David, Douglas Mawson, and Raymond

By opting for Manchurian ponies instead of the dogs recommended by Nansen, Shackleton (opposite) made a mistake repeated three years later by Scott. He reckoned that a pony can pull 2000 pounds and needs 11 pounds of food a day, while a dog pulls 110 pounds and eats 1.5 pounds per day. What he did not allow for is that ponies sink in deep snow and are very vulnerable in blizzards: their sweat covers their bodies and freezes into a coating of ice. Dogs sweat only through their tongues, and can sleep outside in blizzard conditions of −40°. These illustrations are of the voyage of the *Nimrod* to the Antarctic in 1907 (above) and the expedition party of the *Nimrod* in 1909 (left).

Priestley; and the destination, McMurdo Sound. At this point Scott intervened, insisting that his former lieutenant find another base: McMurdo Sound was his prerogative.

The *Nimrod* headed instead for the Bay of Whales, an indentation at the foot of the Ross Ice Shelf, arriving at the end of January 1908 to find it blocked by ice. Shackleton tried to land further west on King Edward VII Land but the density of the ice pack prevented him. He was obliged to make McMurdo Sound his base. Scott never forgave him.

The Attempt on the Pole: 1800 Miles to Cover on Foot in an Unknown Region

Transport, provisions, and men had first to be chosen. Nansen had recommended dogs. Shackleton opted to buy Manchurian ponies: six out of ten died before

The team that attempted to reach the geographic South Pole returned on the *Nimrod*: from left to right are Frank Wild, Ernest Shackleton, Eric Marshall, and Jameson Adams.

setting out, and the men were left to pull the sleds.

Provisions were more satisfactory. Remembering that he had nearly died of scurvy, which he attributed to poor nutrition, Shackleton drew up the rations with medical advice: seal meat while wintering, pemmican and biscuits (2 pounds per person per day) on the march.

By the end of November Shackleton had beaten Scott's record and discovered the Beardmore Glacier. This long, gentle slope of 125 miles, rising to an altitude of 6500 feet, gave ready access to the Antarctic plateau.

"A Live Donkey Is Better Than a Dead Lion"

With these words to his wife, Emily, Shackleton explained why, on 9 January 1909, miles from the Pole, he had decided to turn back. The men were exhausted and short of food. The outward journey had taken seventy days, and the return took fifty. And the *Nimrod*, under orders to leave no later than 1 March to avoid being trapped by ice, was no longer there.

The ship was 20 miles to the north, in McMurdo Sound, and there was little hope on board of seeing Shackleton's party again. Volunteers made plans to spend the winter there, if only to recover the bodies. Then they sighted a column of smoke: Shackleton had set fire to a hut in order to signal their presence. An additional triumph was that David, Mawson, and Mackay, whose mission had been to explore Victoria Land, had reached the South Magnetic Pole.

Scott vs. Amundsen: The Race to the South Pole

On his return to England on 14 June 1909 Shackleton was acclaimed a hero by public and press, and

Shackleton discovered a glacier and called it Beardmore after the English industrialist who backed his expedition. The mountain range bordering the glacier's west face he named after Queen Alexandra (Victoria) who had given him the British flag to raise on the South Pole. The team did not reach its goal, but the flag was nonetheless erected 97 miles from the Pole. The occasion is recorded in the photograph above.

"For sudden the worst turns the best to the brave."
Robert Browning

knighted, at the age of thirty-six, by King Edward VII.

Resenting Shackleton's success, Scott resolved to undertake another expedition. Circumstances, however, were against him. There was rumor of war in Europe, and the Admiralty preferred to invest in armaments. The scientific institutions, normally well funded, were short on financial backers.

Only public opinion seemed to be on the side of adventure. Taking a gamble, Scott announced his project in *The Times.* A national subscription was organized and the total made up by official grants. The expedition became reality, but on a tight budget.

Scott Set Out at Last...and So Did Amundsen

Scott was aboard the *Terra Nova,* an old Scottish whaler, with sixty-five men (fifty of them on a temporary assignment from the navy), seventeen ponies, and thirty dogs. He also took three motorized sleds, tested by Charcot in the Col du Lautaret. Preparations had lasted nearly a year. The expedition had two aims: scientific study and, of course, the conquest of the South Pole. There Scott was to meet Amundsen, a formidable rival.

With Nansen's support, Amundsen had been preparing another drifting expedition in the Arctic in the *Fram,* aiming to start at the Bering Strait and cross the North Pole.

The *Terra Nova* (opposite) set sail on 1 June 1910 under the command of Edward Evans, a lieutenant whom Scott had promoted. Scott himself joined the expedition at Simonstown, South Africa. In the meantime Cecil Henry Meares had gone to Siberia to buy thirty dogs and seventeen ponies. He had much experience with dogs and picked them well; however, he knew nothing of ponies and chose poorly. Captain Titus Oates realized this, too late, but he did his best to prepare them for the attempt on the Pole.

However, in September 1909, following the competing claims of Cook and Peary and the withdrawal of some of his backers, Amundsen decided to modify this plan: he would certainly make the drifting trip in the Arctic, but first he would spend a year in the Antarctic. There was nothing strange about this: the route from

Europe to the Bering Strait passed Cape Horn, as the Panama Canal was not yet in existence.

Amundsen wanted to be first to reach the South Pole. However, knowing that he would be in competition with Scott, he judged it wise to say nothing and avoid political complications between England and Norway.

In June 1910 the *Fram* officially left for the Bering Strait.

"Beg Leave Inform You Proceeding Antarctic"

Then this telegram was sent by Amundsen to Scott from Madeira. Amundsen also wrote to the king of Norway and Nansen informing them of the change of program. Scott was enraged.

On 14 January 1911 Amundsen landed. He prepared to winter with eight companions and 116 dogs at Framheim, a base set up at the Bay of Whales on the Ross Ice Shelf.

A week earlier Scott had moored the *Terra Nova* in McMurdo Sound. His plans were ambitious: to survey the terrain with his team of scientists, to reach the South Pole with a select band of men, and to leave a third party, commanded by Campbell, wintering on King Edward VII Land.

The March to the South Pole

That autumn Amundsen deposited caches of supplies in three places, at latitudes of 80°, 81°, and 82°S.

In the spring he chose those who would accompany him to the Pole: Helmer Hanssen, a seasoned officer

The Framheim Base (below) was built by Amundsen (above) and his colleagues on the Bay of Whales in ten days. There were fourteen similar tents housing dogs, supplies, and coal. Polheim (right), the tent that Amundsen left in place, proved to be 1.67 miles from the geographic South Pole.

who had been with him in the Northwest Passage and was experienced with dogs; Sverre Hassel, a customs officer and sled driver; Olav Bjaaland, a ski champion; and Oscar Wisting, a harpooner of whales.

On 20 October 1911 they left Framheim Base with twelve dogs to pull each sled. On 17 November they reached the foot of a mountain range at 85°S, having covered 15 miles per day without undue effort. Ahead of them lay a trip of almost 700 miles to the Pole and back.

There followed a terrifying ascent of the Axel Heiberg Glacier, riddled with crevasses. At the top Amundsen kept eighteen dogs for three sleds and ordered that the remainder be killed. By 10 December they were only 68 miles from the Pole. The altitude was decreasing.

On 14 December Amundsen and his companions reached the mythical 90°. For three days they measured the altitude of the sun with the sextant, which neither Peary nor Cook had done at the North Pole. Before departing, Amundsen left a letter for Scott.

On 25 January 1912 the team was back again in Framheim, victorious. The return journey had taken just ninety-six days.

At Framheim (opposite below) the Norwegians gave the finishing touches to their equipment, reduced loads, and trained dogs. Amundsen, although autocratic by temperament, bowed to democratic rules and created a good team spirit.

"I have never known any man to be placed in such a diametrically opposite position to the goal of his desires as I at that moment. The regions around the North Pole—well, yes, the North Pole itself—had attracted me from childhood, and here I was at the South Pole. Can anything more topsy-turvy be imagined?"
Roald Amundsen
The South Pole, 1912

A Winter at Cape Evans

S cott's base at Cape Evans (left) and (inset) Scott at work. The winter team consisted of a general staff of fifteen, plus nine petty officers and sailors. In the true hierarchical spirit of the Royal Navy, officers and scientists had one messhall, and the crew members were allocated separate quarters. Progress and discoveries were made in several fields: meteorology and glaciology (thanks to Simpson and Priestley), as well as geology and cartography. Wilson, Apsley, Cherry-Garrard, and Henry Bowers braved bitter temperatures to bring back embryos of emperor penguins. No one had studied these creatures, seen as the possible missing link between reptiles and birds. Scott gave such weight to the scientific program that he underestimated the difficulties of reaching the Pole. Though he was surrounded by brave men, he lacked the experience of an Amundsen.

Festivities at the Base

On 22 June 1911 Scott and his general staff celebrated Midwinter's Day, as was the tradition in Antarctic bases. Seated, from left to right, are Debenham, Oates, Meares, Bowers, Cherry-Garrard, Scott, Wilson, Simpson, Nelson, Evans, Day, and Taylor. Standing: on the left, Wright and Atkinson; on the right, Gran. The menu included seal consommé, and the meal was generously washed down with generous quantities of Bordeaux and champagne. The engraving of Napoleon on the left wall—obviously unusual in British circles—had been brought by Captain Oates, a keen admirer of the emperor.

Bitter Victory

This photograph was meant to represent victory. Misfortune had dogged Scott (standing center) and his companions (left to right) Wilson, Evans, Oates, and Bowers. In the tent Amundsen had left they had just found a letter:

"Dear Captain Scott, As you probably are the first to reach this area after us, I will ask you kindly to forward this letter to King Haakon VII [of Norway]. If you can use any of the articles left in the tent, please do not hesitate to do so. With kind regards. I wish you a safe return.
Yours truly,
Roald Amundsen"

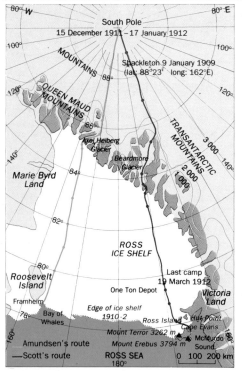

Meanwhile Scott and His Men Forged Ahead

On 10 December 1911 all reached the Beardmore
Glacier. Exhausted by the powdery snow, the ponies
were encrusted in frozen sweat. Scott ordered
their slaughter. The loads were divided between three
sleds, four men to each. The climb began. They were
480 miles from the Pole. It took eleven days to ascend
the glacier. Scott sent back the last support team,
choosing four men to accompany him: Wilson, Oates,
Bowers, and Edgar Evans.

On 9 January 1912 they reached 88°23'5", the
latitude at which Shackleton had turned back exactly
three years earlier. They pressed on. A week later
Bowers sighted a black flag tied to the runner of a sled.

"The causes of the
disaster are not due to
faulty organization, but
to misfortune in all risks
that had to be
undertaken."

Robert Scott
Message to the public
March 1912

"The Worst Has Happened"

Scott's diary, 16 January 1912: "The worst has happened, or nearly the worst.... The Norwegians have forestalled us and are first at the Pole.... Tomorrow we must march on to the Pole and then hasten home with all the speed we can compass."

The return journey started well. A south wind allowed a sail to be fitted to the sled—which would make traveling easier—but all the men were suffering. Evans was exhausted, Oates' feet were frost-bitten. On 17 February Evans died after a fall. On 16 March, the day before his thirty-second birthday, Oates realized gangrene had overcome him, and he went out into the raging blizzard, never to return.

"I am just going outside and may be some time." These were Titus Oates' last words to his companions when he decided to meet his death in a blizzard rather than hold up the rest of the party. The painting above is a tribute to his courage.

On 19 March Scott, Wilson, and Bowers were within 11 miles of One Ton Depot but could go no further. "For four days we have been unable to leave the tent—the gale howling about us."

The following November a search party found the bodies of the three men, with Scott's papers and diaries.

Australians in the Antarctic: The Mawson Expedition

Douglas Mawson, an Australian born in 1882, had been pressed to join Scott in 1910 but he decided instead to organize his own expedition, financed by Australian businessmen.

Mawson left Hobart aboard the *Aurora* on 2 December 1911. He sailed along the ice pack and, a little short of Terre Adélie, dropped anchor at Cape Denison. Eighteen men landed on this desert of ice, which was swept by gales and blizzards for an average of 285 days every year.

Leaving Mawson ashore, the *Aurora* sailed west. A second team of eight men led by Frank Wild charted 285 miles of coast, incidentally discovering a great emperor penguin rookery that fascinated the biologists, near Hasswell Island.

Several parties set out in the spring. One went in search of the Magnetic Pole, and a second headed west across Terre Adélie, finding only a wasteland of ice. Three others—Mawson; Xavier Mertz, ski champion; and Bes Ninnis, a British officer—went east.

Progress over the glaciers was slow. On 12 December, as Mertz and Mawson were negotiating a crevasse, they suddenly realized that it had engulfed Ninnis with his sled and dogs, their tent, and most of the food. All cries went unanswered.

The two men were left 310 miles from base with only ten days' worth of provisions and nothing to feed the dogs. The six huskies were eaten one by one. Mertz died of exhaustion. Mawson pressed on alone, having

On 14 December 1912 Ninnis disappeared into a crevasse with his sled and dogs. For three hours Mawson shouted desperately into the depths hoping to locate him. The only sign of life was a dog moaning 145 feet below. Powerless, all that Mawson (above) could do was say some final prayers for his companion.

harnessed himself to half a sled. At one point the snow suddenly gave way beneath his weight, but, miraculously, the harness held him fast, and he summoned the strength to pull himself to the surface.

On 1 February he finally reached base. The *Aurora,* obeying his instructions, had just set off, leaving six men to wait for him. The boat was summoned by radio, which Mawson had introduced to the Antarctic, but a blizzard prevented its return, and the men were forced to spend another winter there. The *Aurora* collected them in December 1913.

Mawson and one of his men (above) struggle against the blizzard in Terre Adélie to cut ice for their water supplies.

Shackleton's Second Expedition: The Story of the *Endurance*

Early in 1912 the world learned of Amundsen's conquest of the South Pole. There was no news of Robert Scott, whose tragic end was not discovered until November.

Shackleton, Scott's former rival, decided to undertake another British expedition. His plan was to cross Antarctica from the Weddell Sea to the Ross Sea via the South Pole, a distance of 2050 miles. Shackleton allowed 120 days for the journey, even more taxing than those undertaken by Amundsen and Scott. He took with him five men and fifty-four dogs.

As the *Endurance* was ready to sail, war broke out in Europe. It was August 1914. Shackleton hesitated about leaving, but Winston Churchill gave the order to proceed.

Reaching South Georgia in early November, Shackleton had to wait there a month: the ice pack extended very far north that year. He sailed on 5 December and spent five weeks seeking lanes of open water between the coast and the ice fields.

On 10 January the *Endurance* arrived in Coats Land, on the shores of the Wendell Sea, where ice cliffs towered 70 feet high, making landing impossible. Blizzards and gales ensued, and "a survey of the position on the 20th showed that the ship was firmly [stuck]. The ice was packed heavily and firmly all round the *Endurance* in every direction as far as the eye could reach from the masthead." It was the middle of the Antarctic summer, and there was absolutely no escape from the ice.

Frank Hurley, the expedition photographer, used a flash to take this dramatic picture of the *Endurance* trapped in the ice. The boat held out against the tremendous pressure for many months.

Nine Months Adrift in Search of Open Water

From 20 January to 27 October 1915 the *Endurance* drifted with the ice pack at about 6 miles per day. The twenty-eight men on board hunted seals and penguins, competing with killer whales for their quarry. There was anxious talk of the war, about which no clear details were known.

After a fairly easy winter the melting waters of the spring brought problems: pressure ridges formed in the ice, endangering—and ultimately crushing —the ship. On 27 October Shackleton gave the order to abandon ship. The men headed for Paulet Island, 355 miles north-northwest across the pack. Progress was wretched: just over 11 miles in one week, wading through deep snow. Shackleton decided to give up and drift on a large, solid ice floe. This continued from November 1915 to the following April.

Frank Hurley, the expedition photographer, recounted that on 8 April 1916: "Shortly after 6 p.m. the watchman raised the alarm that the floe was splitting. Our camp was reduced to an overcrowded rocking triangle, and it was evident that we must take the first opportunity to escape, no matter how desperate the chances might be."

Shackleton divided his men among three boats. He, Frank Wild, and eleven others went aboard the *James Caird*, the larger whaler. Frank Worsley and nine men took the smaller one, and Crean and three men had the little dinghy.

They advanced by oar and by sail, but most of all with the current. On 13 April they at last reached open water near Elephant Island and were able to land: solid

"Two massive floes, miles of ice, jammed her sides and held her fast, while the third floe tore across her stern, ripping off the rudder as though it had been made of matchwood. She quivered and groaned as rudder and sternpost were torn off, and part of her keel was driven upwards by the ice. The shock of the impact was indescribable. To us it was as though the whole world were in the throes of an earthquake."
Frank Worsley
Endurance, 1931

ground for the first time in twenty months. However, winter was looming. No one would look for them there, and Shackleton was uncertain they could survive on seals and penguins. He decided to venture forth in search of help.

Six Men in a Boat in the Storms: The Odyssey of the *James Caird*

Taking Worsley, the commander of the *Endurance*, Chief Officer Crean, the carpenter MacNeish, and two sailors, MacCarthy and Vincent, Shackleton headed back for South Georgia, 900 miles east-northeast. He reached his destination under sail on this 22-foot whaleboat with a two-ton ballast. However, storms thrust him to the wild, southern shore of the island, rather than the north coast where whaling stations could have given immediate help.

"9 May: Just after 6 P.M., in the dark, as the boat was in the yeasty backwash from the seas flung from this iron-bound coast, then, just when things looked their worst, they changed for the best. I have

"I had all sails set, and the *James Caird* quickly dipped the beach and its line of dark figures. The westerly wind took us rapidly to the line of pack.... The tale of the next sixteen days is one of supreme strife amid heaving waters.... Cramped in our narrow quarters and continually wet by the spray, we suffered severely from cold throughout the journey."
Ernest Shackleton
South, 1919

marveled often at the thin line that divides success from failure and the sudden turn that leads from apparently certain disaster to comparative safety," wrote Shackleton.

Their water long finished, the six men were desperately thirsty. "We heard a gurgling sound that was sweet music to our ears, and, peering around, found a stream of fresh water almost at our feet.... It was a splendid moment."

South Georgia is a piece of the Alps transplanted to the Atlantic, with peaks, glaciers, and frozen lakes. On 19 May Shackleton set out with two men, three days' supplies, and one rope. The weather was good, the moon full.

The three walked for thirty-six hours across glaciers and crevasses. On Saturday 20 May they heard the siren summoning the Stromness whaling station to work. Shackleton, his emaciated face now overgrown by his beard, approached the Norwegian manager of the station:

"'My name is Shackleton,' I said. Immediately he put

"Our meals were regular...this point was essential, since the conditions of the voyage made increasing calls upon our vitality. Breakfast, at 8 A.M., consisted of a [small cup] of hot hoosh made from Bovril ration, two biscuits, and some lumps of sugar. Lunch came at 1 P.M., and comprised Bovril ration, eaten raw, and a [small cup] of hot milk for each man. Tea, at 5 P.M., had the same menu. The meals were the bright beacons in those cold and stormy days. The glow of warmth and comfort produced by the food and drink made optimists of us all."
Shackleton, *South*, 1919

out his hand and said,

'Come in. Come in.'

'Tell me, when was the war over?' I asked.

'The war is not over,' he answered. 'Millions are being killed. Europe is mad. The world is mad.'"

Six Men Safe, Twenty-Two Still To Be Rescued

Worsley immediately set out to fetch the three men left behind on the south coast. Meanwhile, Shackleton equipped a whaler to return to Elephant Island. On Tuesday morning he set sail on the *Southern Sky,* but the ice pack blocked his passage, and he was forced to turn back.

Shackleton did not give up. The Uruguayan government lent him a trawler—in vain. He then went to Punta Arenas (Chile) and chartered a schooner from the British community. Again stopped by the ice pack, he headed for the Falklands.

It was the end of July 1916 and mid-winter. An English relief ship, the *Discovery,* was expected in mid-September. However, there was no question of Shackleton waiting: his men had to be rescued at once. On 25 August Shackleton finally recovered the rest of his crew aboard a small Chilean steamer.

Years later, in 1956, the geologist Raymond Priestley, who had wintered with Scott and Shackleton before meeting Amundsen, summed up the respective merits of the three explorers. As leader of a scientific expedition he recommended Scott; for a swift and efficient attempt on the Pole Amundsen was the man; but in the face of adversity with no salvation in sight, the answer was to pray for the arrival of Shackleton.

Contrary to Expectations, Reaching the South Pole by Air Proved Scarcely Easier Than by Foot

Although airships and airplanes crossed the Arctic skies, few were tempted by aerial exploration of the South Pole. There were no manned bases and no airfields but plenty of permanent winds and altitudes

H ubert Wilkins (below) obtained substantial financial backing for his expedition from the press magnate Randolph Hearst. This enabled him to buy two up-to-date Lockheed Vegas. His first flight took place on 16 November 1928, when he became the first man to fly over the Antarctic.

of up to 13,000 feet. Above all, distances were huge between the Antarctic and the nearest supply points.

The first to make the attempt was an Australian, Hubert Wilkins, who in 1928 took off from Deception Island. On his return from the 1300-mile journey, he announced that Graham Land was separated from the Antarctic continent by several straits, a statement that proved to be untrue.

The same year, American Commander Richard E. Byrd, on a private expedition, wintered in the Bay of Whales on the Ross Ice Shelf. He called his base Little America. Five American expeditions set out from here between 1929 and 1956. The 1929 flight over the route taken by Amundsen brought no new discoveries. However, on later journeys by air and by sled the geologist Lawrence Gould discovered and studied the Rockefeller Mountains, named after one of the expedition's patrons. Byrd returned in 1934 and systematically explored the east coast of the Ross Ice Shelf, till then completely unknown.

Between 1933 and 1936 American explorer Lincoln Ellsworth, who had flown with Amundsen in the Arctic, made the first flight across the Antarctic: 2300 miles from Graham Land to Little America.

Aboard his three-engine Ford, the *Floyd Bennett*, Richard E. Byrd flew over the South Pole along the route taken by Amundsen, who advised him. The expedition, comprising three airplanes, ninety-five dogs, and over fifty men, reached the Ross Ice Shelf on Christmas Day 1928. The base, Little America, was set up, and the flight to the South Pole took place on 28 November 1929 after several reconnaissance trips. In 15 hours, 51 minutes, Byrd covered the distance that had taken Amundsen three months on foot.

Daring exploits have been followed by scientific work. In the past fifty years polar exploration has benefited from scientific and technical progress, and new factors—notably oil, ocean transport, environmental concerns, and defense—have come into play. Extensive multi-national research projects have been conducted in both the north and south polar regions.

CHAPTER V
THE POLES AT STAKE

Space exploration has revolutionized methods of observing the poles. The image on the right was taken by the satellite *Nimbus 5*. It shows the sea ice surrounding Antarctica on a winter's day.

The Inland Ice Sheet That Covers Most of Greenland's 770,000 Square Miles Has Been the Subject of Scientific Study Since 1930

Greenland had been crossed by Nansen and Peary on skis; the ethnologist Knud Rasmussen had explored the northeast coast with dogsleds; and in 1912 a Swiss glaciologist, de Quervain, took the first measurements of temperature and snow accumulation.

In 1930 Coste and Bellonte made the first nonstop flight from Paris to New York. The most direct path, now standard for transatlantic flights, passes over Greenland and requires a knowledge of atmospheric conditions.

Eager to establish the route, the Germans organized a scientific expedition directed by geophysicist and meteorologist Alfred Wegener, father of the theory of continental drift. The object was to set up a meteorological and glaciological research station, Eismitte, 250 miles from the coast, at an altitude of 9800 feet, backed up by weather stations on the east and west coasts.

In April 1930 Wegener landed on the west coast, north of Disko Island, with 100 tons of goods. Johannes Georgi and Ernest Sorge installed themselves at Eismitte that summer, while Wegener's men supplied the station from the west coast, with the help of Eskimos.

Wegener made a last trip to the station at the end of October, which was very late in the season, accompanied only by Dr. Loewe and an Eskimo, Rasmus. The temperature was already –50°. Loewe, his feet frostbitten, realized he had gangrene. Amputation being the only hope, Georgi operated with what he had on hand.

While Loewe's life was saved, he was not able to continue the trip. He remained at Eismitte, where there was enough food for one extra mouth.

In 1906 Alfred Wegener, a twenty-six-year-old scientist, took part in Mylius Erichsen's Danish expedition to the northeast coast of Greenland. Despite the tragic deaths of Erichsen and two companions, the team produced many maps of new ground. Wegener discovered Queen Louise Land. In 1912–3 he crossed Greenland from east to west on sleds pulled by ponies. The picture below shows him on his last expedition in 1930, using a drill to measure the annual accumulation of snow.

Wegener and his guide, Rasmus, decided to set out for the west coast with only seventeen dogs to accompany them. It was a fateful journey—one from which they were never to return.

The following spring Wegener's body was found, 117 miles from the coast. Its resting place was marked by a ski standing like a cross in the snow. Of Rasmus, who had buried his companion, nothing was ever heard again.

The first of the French polar expeditions set out from Port Victor in autumn 1948.

Wegener's project at Eismitte was carried on by the French, under the direction of Paul-Emile Victor. Ponies and huskies were replaced by machines, and aiplanes would fly in at low altitude to deliver food and fuel.

In 1950 and 1951 two teams led by Robert Guillard and Paul-Emile Voguet wintered there; and in the summer geophysicists did 400 seismic shots at ten-mile intervals. (Seismic shooting is a method of geophysical prospecting.)

In 1952 Victor negotiated the use of the American military base at Thule for an expedition of 1240 miles across the far north of Greenland. It was led by Guillard and followed the routes taken by Peary and Rasmussen.

Queen Elizabeth II and Prime Minister Sir Winston Churchill were patrons of an expedition led by Commander Simpson to a particularly inaccessible region of Greenland, mostly cut off by ice, even in summer. The base, North Ice, was built on Lake Britannia 250 miles from the coast. Sunderland flying boats were used to bring supplies from further south. For two years (1952–4), British teams wintered there and in the summer traveled to Thule, carrying out seismic, altimetric, and gravimetric surveys.

The International Glaciological Expedition in Greenland

Five countries collaborated on a survey to

Paul-Emile Victor (left) first went to Greenland in 1934 with Charcot and the *Pourquoi-Pas?* He was an indefatigable promoter of expeditions to Greenland and Terre Adélie. Among the many scientists and technicians he recruited was Robert Guillard (below), now the most experienced French explorer, a veteran of forty-four expeditions.

establish whether the inland ice sheet in Greenland was stable, retreating, or advancing. This project required repeated measurements to be taken over a number of years and was beyond the resources of any individual country. The French were in charge of the organization, cooperating with the Danish, Swiss, Austrians, and Germans.

Two ships, two airplanes, two helicopters, and numerous snow tractors took part, while scientists from the five countries sought to establish the ebb and flow in the mass of the ice cap.

The loss comes from the melting of the névé (granular snow from the surface of the upper end of a glacier) in coastal regions at an altitude below 4800 feet and from the volume of icebergs calved by glaciers. The gain comes from the annual snowfall in the central region. It is not yet technically possible to establish whether the volume of ice in Greenland is increasing or decreasing. We do know, however, that were it to melt entirely, the sea level would rise by some 23 feet.

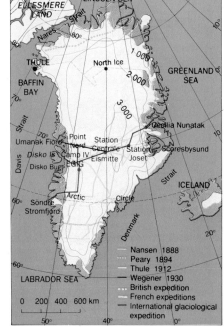

Ethnologists Study the Inuit Civilization

Knud Rasmussen was the first to take an interest in these Eskimo people. With his friend Peter Freuchen, he founded a private bank in 1910 in the Inuits' capital, the village of Upernavik, and gave it the mythical name of Thule. The aim was to regulate the fur trade and protect the Eskimos from ruthless exploitation by whalers and the occasional explorer.

He also organized expeditions to study the history and way of life of the Inuits. He examined their methods of hunting and of transport and their use of dogs and sleds. On his most famous expedition, Thule V (1923–4), he crossed the Northwest Passage to study Eskimo groups between Thule and Alaska. His work has been continued by others, including the Frenchman Jean Malaurie, whose book, *The Last Kings of Thule*, has helped to make the Inuits recognized throughout the world.

Exploration of the Arctic Ocean

Nansen's long drift in 1895 was a first step in the study of the Arctic Ocean, subsequently pursued by the Soviets with more modern methods: there seems little reason to immobilize a ship and crew when an airplane can land on the ice pack and leave a team to establish

Ivan Papanin (1895–1986, above) when the first drifting observatory, Severny Poloius, was evacuated in 1938. Undoubtedly the most popular polar figure in the USSR, he was director of the Northern Sea Route from 1939 to 1945, when he was promoted to rear admiral. From 1955 on he worked tirelessly to promote Soviet expeditions in the Antarctic.

a drifting station, propelled by wind, current, and tide.

In May 1937 four Soviet airplanes took off from Rudolf Island in the Franz Josef archipelago and landed by the Pole, depositing four men to set up a station there: Ivan Papanin, the expedition leader, Ivan Shirchov, an oceanographer, Gueni Fedorov, a geophysicist, and Ernest Krenkel, the radio operator. For nine months they drifted south on the ice pack, covering a few miles per day. They were picked up at the end of February 1938 near the east coast of Greenland, having taken soundings of the sea bottom and collected valuable meteorological and oceanographic data.

The principle of a drifting observatory was applied again in 1950 and 1951 by Mikhail Somov and A. F. Treshnikov, with SP2 and SP3. The longest-lasting station of the kind operated from 1973 to 1981 and involved 1500 people. Automatic stations were also established at this period by both Soviets and Americans.

New Vehicles of Exploration: Icebreakers, Satellites, and Nuclear Submarines

The *Nautilus* led the way in 1958 when it crossed the Arctic in ninety-nine hours. Six months later, in March 1959, the *Skate* surfaced at the Pole, and in 1962 the Soviets arrived in the *Leninski Komsomolets*. The British made the crossing in the *Dreadnought* in 1971. Little is known of the results of these submarine journeys: the Arctic is an ideal site for secret military experiments as the ice prevents detection by satellite, and the constant collisions of the ice pack create a disturbance that hinders the detection of submarines. Certain data has nonetheless been made public, such as the depth of the sea bottom.

For some years an extensive international operation, Mizex (Marginal Ice Zone Experiment), has engaged in a scientific study of the interaction of ice, atmosphere,

Knud Rasmussen (1879–1933) was the son of a Danish pastor who settled on the west coast of Greenland. After a childhood spent playing with the Eskimo children and driving dogsleds, he became professor of Greenlandic at the University of Copenhagen. Early on he decided to devote himself to ethnological and archaeological studies of the different Eskimo tribes, which he financed from the profits of his bank at Thule.

and oceans, specifically in the Greenland Sea.

In 1977 the first ship reached the North Pole: the *Arktika,* the most powerful icebreaker in the world. The following year its sister ship, the *Sibir,* escorting a freighter, opened a passage north of all the Siberian islands and established a new ocean route.

Following in the Footsteps of the Early 20th-Century Explorers

The Englishman Wally Herbert set out with three companions to cross the Arctic Ocean with dogsleds. He was seeking both adventure and scientific discovery. The journey from Point Barrow in Alaska to Spitsbergen via the North Pole took from 21 February 1968 to 29 May 1969 and covered 2170 miles as the crow flies. However, the actual distance was over 3700 miles, since the team encountered many huge ridges of ice.

For half of the sixteen months the expedition was unable to advance: in summer because of the moving ice floes, in winter because of darkness and cold. The four men spent these periods studying patterns of air, water, and ice on what was effectively a drifting observatory.

The Challenge of the North Pole

Like mountains and the sea, the North Pole draws

adventurous spirits, and in increasing numbers. It can now be reached by airplanes, bringing supplies and, if necessary, rescue.

In 1978 the Japanese climber Naome Uemura made a solo expedition to the North Pole with a sled and seventeen dogs, resupplied five times by a twin-engine Otter. He left Cape Columbia on 6 March and reached the Pole on 29 April. He took fifty-eight days to cover a distance that must actually have been much more than the 480 miles indicated on the maps—this party, too, was confronted by many ridges of ice.

The next year a Soviet expedition undertook an even greater challenge: to reach the North Pole from Henrietta Island 930 miles away in the north-east of the New Siberian archipelago. Six men, commanded by Dimitri Shparo, set out without dogs or sleds, each carrying a 100-pound backpack. They left on 16 March 1979 and took seventy-six days to ski to the Pole. It was the end of May when they arrived, with channels of melted water hindering their progress.

In 1986 two expeditions left from Cape Columbia for the Pole. The American Will Steger wanted to repeat Peary's journey without stopping for supplies. His team of five men and one woman set out on 8 March with dogsleds. They reached the Pole on 1 May—a fifty-six day march instead of the thirty-six claimed by Peary.

On 9 March, a day after Steger left, a young French doctor, Jean-Louis Etienne, set out alone on skis, pulling a 90-pound sled. Fresh supplies were flown to him every two weeks. After a month the two expeditions ran into each other. Each pressed on separately, and on 11 May Dr. Etienne reached the Pole.

The Arctic is in the Hands of the Americans and the Russians

The Americans and the Russians control the straits: the Bering Strait on the one side, the Barents Sea

In March 1959 the *Skate* (left), an American nuclear submarine, surfaced at the North Pole. It used a sounder to measure the depth of the ice before emerging.

on the other. They exploit the vast natural resources of the region: oil at Prudhoe Bay on the north coast of Alaska and natural gas in northwest Siberia, close to the Arctic Circle, especially around Urengoy.

The Northeast Passage is used more extensively today than is the Northwest Passage. The Russians alone, with the largest fleet of icebreakers in the world, are responsible for an annual traffic of four million tons. Siberia thus takes on an economic and strategic role.

These developments are not without adverse effects on the environment and the life of the Arctic peoples, making a collaboration between Soviets and Americans there and at the opposite end of the world all the more desirable. Of course, such a collaboration now stands a substantially greater chance in light of recent political developments.

Jean-Louis Etienne (left) en route to the North Pole in 1986. He had carefully trained to build up resistance to the cold.

A 20,000-ton, 75,000-horsepower icebreaker the *Arktika* (right) left Murmansk on 9 August 1977. Passing north of Novaya Zemlya, it rounded Cape Chelyuskin and headed directly north to reach the Pole on 17 August. Guided by two helicopters, it crossed areas that had been frozen for some years, its speed never exceeding 2 knots. On 23 August the ship was back at Murmansk, having proved that a ship can cross the Arctic Ocean by routes other than the Northeast and Northwest Passages.

After the Second World War the American Navy Embarked on a Campaign of Aerial Photography of the Antarctic

In 1946 Admiral Byrd, a seasoned polar explorer, launched Operation Highjump, the largest expedition ever sent to Antarctica—it involved an aircraft carrier, six special-purpose aircraft, several icebreakers, numerous auxiliary ships, and four thousand men. Many photographs were taken, but they could not be used for maps, as checkpoints were not available on the ground.

The first maps were produced by Operation Windmill (1947–8), part of the larger operation, and covered a small section of the coast west of Terre Adélie, where ten years later the Soviets set up their Mirny Base.

Terre Adélie Became the First French Base

In 1947 Paul-Emile Victor was preparing to go to
Greenland, funded by the government, when three
young explorers, Yves Vallette, Robert Pommier, and
Jacques-André Martin, suggested an expedition to Terre
Adélie. Victor, who was enthusiastic about the project,
managed to obtain additional financing. The French
polar expeditions were born.

Victor found a ship for the expedition in California
and renamed it *Commandant-Charcot*. The French
Navy equipped it in St. Malo and put Captain Max
Douguet in command.

At the end of December 1949 the *Charcot* sailed
south from Hobart, and a week later came into sight of
the ice pack, glowing white on the horizon.

After two weeks negotiating the ice, the ship moored
near Cap de la Découverte and landed the first expedition of eleven men led by André Liotard. They wintered at Port Martin, a base named after Jacques-André
Martin, who had died on the crossing, and started work
on a map of Terre Adélie. In the spring a large rookery
of emperor penguins was discovered at Pointe Géologie.

In 1950 the *Charcot* landed a second expedition at
Port Martin. There were seventeen men under the
command of Michel Barré, among them Dr. Loewe,
who had been in Greenland with Wegener, and
Bertrand Imbert, who was to direct the International
Geophysical Year.

The team continued its investigations in geophysics
and the natural sciences, and Pierre Mayaud
determined the position of the South Magnetic Pole. As
it happened, this was the last winter at the base, which
was destroyed by fire on 23 January 1952 in the space
of a few hours.

Later French bases were positioned further west at
Pointe Géologie, where, on a third expedition led by
Mario Marret in 1952, valuable work was done by Dr.
Jean Rivolier and the ornithologist Jean Prévost on
emperor penguins.

The greatest threat to
all polar bases is fire.
At Port Martin (above)
in 1952 the blizzard
rendered vain all efforts
to extinguish the flames,
and the members of the
expedition, fortunately
unhurt, could do nothing
but watch. Byrd had a
similar experience in the
1930s, as, more recently,
did the Soviets.

The population of emperor penguins is estimated at 400,000, though new colonies may yet be discovered. One was found in 1986 on the eastern shore of the Weddell Sea.

Norwegians, Swedish, British, and Australians Established Bases in the Antarctic

An international expedition made up of Norwegian, Swedish, and British scientists spent two continuous winters at Maudheim, on the Atlantic side of Antarctica. Under the direction of John Giaever, geological, meteorological, glaciological, and seismic studies were carried out, gathering useful data.

Two years later, in 1954, the Australians formed the Australian National Antarctic Research Expeditions (ANARE), directed by Phillip Law, and established a base named Mawson in MacRobertson Land (62°52'E) by the Lambert Glacier, an immense expanse 430 miles long by 31 miles wide.

During the International Geophysical Year (1957–8) Twelve Countries Combined Their Observations

The International Geophysical Year (IGY) helped to bring together the information gathered by the various countries involved in polar research. Scientists no longer had to work in isolation but could share their findings in such areas as glaciology and meteorology.

On the initiative of two geophysicists—Sydney Chapman and Lloyd Berkner—following a meeting of the Commission on the Ionosphere, the International Council of Scientific Unions resolved on a program of international cooperation for what was actually a year and a half—from July 1957 to December 1958. This time was chosen to correspond with a period of maximum sunspot activity.

It was in the IGY that the first satellites were launched, *Sputnik* in October 1957 and *Explorer 1* in January 1958. The main thrust of the effort, however, was concentrated on the Antarctic, where twelve countries established forty-eight stations. Four of the countries involved operated bases in the interior of the continent in conditions of extreme cold and peril.

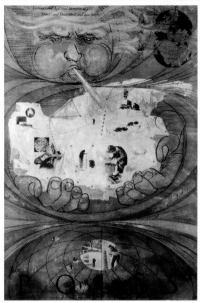

Between 1956 and 1959 Sixty Field Workers and Technicians Operated Two Modern Observatories in Terre Adélie

The Académie des Sciences in France formed a national committee for the IGY under the direction of Pierre Lejay, Jean Coulomb, and André Danjon. Bertrand Imbert was in charge of Antarctic projects, which which drew extensively on the resources of the French polar expeditions.

The *Norsel*, which, with its commander Guttorn Jacobsen, had previously served on the Maudheim expedition, transported men and material to the other side of the world, and carried out important oceanographic work.

Three expeditions were organized. The object of the first, led by Robert Guillard, a veteran of Greenland, was to establish two bases. During the three months of the Antarctic spring in 1956 he set up Charcot, 200 miles to the south at an altitude of 8000 feet. Supplies and equipment had to be transported across crevasses and sastrugi (wind-caused wavelike irregularities in the snow) by snow tractors, over a distance of 1550 miles.

The second expedition, led by Bertrand Imbert, set out in December 1957 and inaugurated the Charcot base. Jacques Dubois, Claude Lorius, and Roland Schlich spent nine months from February to November alone there.

The third expedition was similarly organized under Gaston Rouillon, who had led an expedition in Greenland, the team comprising René Garcia, Guy Ricou, and Henri Larzillière. A shadow was cast by the death of the meteorologist, André Prudhomme, who was lost in a blizzard.

An American Satellite Made the Greatest Discovery of the International Geophysical Year in March 1958

From information brought back by *Explorer 3*, physicist James Van Allen discovered that the earth is encircled by bands of high-energy particles trapped in the terrestial magnetic field at an altitude of 37,200 miles. On the ground, at stations such as Dumont d'Urville situated in the area of maximum auroral activity, it has been possible to record magnetic storms while simultaneously analyzing their visual or radioelectric displays. Measurements taken by satellites in space have made it possible to map the earth's magnetosphere, the space dominated by the planet's magnetic field.

In 1956 Antarctica— Apart from the Pole— Was Still Unexplored

A transantarctic expedition led by Sir

The International Geophysical Year took place from 1957 to 1958. One of its posters is reproduced opposite. The IGY established a spirit of international cooperation between the various Antarctic bases, which daily exchanged information by radio. Below are Gaston Rouillon, who commanded the third expedition in Terre Adélie, Betrand Imbert, director of expeditions in the IGY, and M. Renard, mechanic, conferring after finding the pilot of a helicopter who had crashed on the ice cap in a blizzard. In answer to an SOS sent out by the French, a Soviet polar ship, the *Ob*, was on the point of sending an airplane to the French base Dumont d'Urville when the helicopter wreckage was found. The injured pilot had taken refuge in the emergency tent.

Vivian Fuchs crossed the continent from the Weddell
Sea to McMurdo Sound and took seismic shots every
30 miles and gravity readings every 15 miles, notably at
the Pole, where the ice was 9300 feet deep. The journey
lasted ninety-nine days. Seismic research was also
undertaken by the Americans—who had by far the
largest program in Antarctica—the Soviets, French,
and Japanese.

In the 1960s the American Amory H. Waite used
altimetric airplane radar to measure the depth of
the ice. Aerial expeditions flew over the entire
continent: the British, led by Gordon Robin, covered
the east; the Americans, the west and the Ross Ice
Shelf; and the West Germans, the Filchner and the
Ronne Ice Shelves to the end of the Weddell Sea.
From these measurements the Scott Polar Research
Institute in Cambridge produced the first
glaciological atlas in 1983.

Ice in the Antarctic Represents 70 Percent of the Fresh Water in the World

Ice covers 538,500 square miles with an average
depth of 7200 feet. Were it to melt, the sea level
worldwide would rise by 230 feet. In contrast to
temperate regions, where rainfall sinks into the
ground and joins the rivers, snow in the polar regions
has been accumulating on the surface of the ice cap
for thousands of years. This enormous mass of ice slips
very slowly towards the coast at a rate of about 32 feet
per year at inland locations.

The polar caps thus provide an invaluable source
of information about the climate of the planet.
Laboratory analysis of ice samples allows the
calculation of the temperature and gas content at
the time of precipitation. Few samples have been
obtained at great depth: the most notable, of 800 feet
at Vostok, has been studied for several years by a
Franco-Soviet team directed by Lorius and Kotlyakov.
It amounts to a climatic archive dating back some
200,000 years.

An Uninhabited Expanse for Thousands of Years, the Antarctic Now Is Home to 1000 People

Seventeen countries maintain forty-nine stations in Antactica, and in the summer—with all the various projects being conducted—the population swells. An international committee was established in 1959 to coordinate the work: the Scientific Committee for Antarctic Research (SCAR). Dr. R. M. Laws of Great Britain was elected president of SCAR from 1990 to 1994.

At McMurdo Base, at the foot of the Ross Ice Shelf, the United States has built what constitutes a year-

People have long marveled at the aurora australis, photographed (above) from Halley's geophysical observatory. Halley had, in the 18th century, suggested a link between the aurorae and magnetic storms. It is now known that an aurora is caused by an electric discharge in ionized gas along the planet's magnetic field lines.

round village. Research at the other U.S. stations is supported by air from this central location.

Private Expeditions Continue in Both the Arctic and Antarctic

Two teams recently made the journey to the South Pole in the footsteps of Scott and Amundsen. A party of three Englishmen set out on 3 November 1985. On 11 January 1986 they were welcomed by the Americans at the Amundsen-Scott base.

At the end of 1986 two glaciologists, the Norwegian Monica Kristensen and the British Neil Macintyre, followed Amundsen's route, taking measurements that proved useful in the equipping of satellite *ERS 1*.

The Future of the Antarctic

For over thirty years the Antarctic Treaty has put a halt to territorial claims and prohibited military activity. Legislation has been passed to protect plant and animal life and regulate mining activities.

In 1991 many countries and nongovernment bodies such as Greenpeace agreed to support an outright ban on oil and mineral exploitation in Antarctica, which could endanger the delicate flora and fauna of the continent. They wish to preserve the continent as the largest remaining wilderness in the world and as an important haven for scientific research.

We now know that burning fossil fuels and

Exactly seventy-four years after Scott, Roger Swan, Roger Mear, and Gareth Wood set out from McMurdo Base to follow in his footsteps. Each man (left) pulled a 330-pound sled, with provisions for a seventy-one-day march across the Ross Ice Shelf, the Beardmore Glacier, and the plateau leading to the South Pole. They arrived to find not Amundsen's tent, but the American Amundsen-Scott Base.

deforestation are capable of actually changing the earth's climate in only a few decades through the greenhouse effect (a warming of the earth's surface associated with increased levels of carbon dioxide). If the hole in the fragile ozone layer grows any larger, the impact of the sun's dangerous rays will affect the delicate balance that makes life possible.

To understand these phenomena it is necessary to step up research all over the planet—and particularly in the polar regions—to monitor sea ice and to observe whether the polar ice caps are melting or expanding. A warming of the climate by even a few degrees could cause widespread flooding of coastal areas and would have serious effects on agriculture.

Clearly, the days of the poles as a focus of international competition are past; the time has come for cooperation. We must learn to understand, to treasure, and to preserve our environment.

Scott's hut at Cape Evans (above) stands as a lasting tribute to the heroic age and forms part of the heritage that each member nation of the Scientific Committee for Antarctic Research undertakes to respect.

DOCUMENTS

Journeys to the ends of the earth:
fact and fiction, past and present.

Jules Verne and John Franklin

For a decade the North Pole kept its secret: the tragic end of the dauntless explorer Franklin was not discovered until February 1859. Jules Verne made it the subject of his novel The English at the North Pole, *featuring the adventures of Captain Hatteras.*

· SIR J⸱ FRANKLIN ·

The Story of Sir John Franklin

"You know, I suppose, my good fellows," he said, "the early history of Franklin. He was a cabin boy, like Cook and Nelson, and, after serving during his youth in several great expeditions, he determined, in 1845, to embark on a search for the Northwest Passage. He was in command of the *Erebus* and *Terror*, two ships that had been previously employed in an Arctic expedition undertaken by James Ross.

"Not one of these ill-fated individuals ever returned to their native land, but you may read nearly all their names on the different bays, and capes, and straits, and points, and channels, and islands that are met with in this region.... There were 138 men altogether. The last letters received from Franklin were dated July 12th, 1845, and written from Isle Disco. 'I hope,' he wrote, 'to weigh anchor to-night for Lancaster Sound.' What has happened since his departure from Disco? The last time the ships were seen was in Melville Bay, by the captains of the *Prince of Wales* and the *Enterprise*, two whalers; and since then there has been no word of them. We are able to follow Franklin, however, in some of his subsequent movements. He went to the west, and up Barrow's Strait and Lancaster Sound, as far as Isle Beechey, where he spent the winter of 1845."

"But how was that ascertained?" asked Bell, the carpenter.

"By three graves discovered by the Austin expedition in 1850, in which three of Franklin's sailors were interred; and also by a document found by Lieutenant Hobson, of the *Fox*, which is dated 1848. From this

February 1859: In a cairn on King William Island, Captain McClintock and his men discovered messages left by men on the Franklin expedition. This 19th-century engraving records the occasion.

we learn that, at the close of the winter, the *Erebus* and the *Terror* went up Wellington Channel as far as the 77th parallel; but, instead of continuing their route to the north, which was doubtless found to be impracticable, they returned south."

"And it was their ruin," said a grave voice. "Salvation was in the north."

Everyone turned to see who had spoken. It was Hatteras, leaning against the railing of the poop, who had made this terrible observation.

"There is no doubt," continued the Doctor, "that Franklin's intention was to reach the American coast; but he was overtaken by furious tempests, and both ships got caught in the ice a few miles from this, and were dragged N.N.E. of Point Victory. But the ships

were not abandoned till the 22nd of April, 1848. What happened during those nineteen months, who knows? What did the poor fellows do with themselves all that time?"...

"It was, perhaps, his crew who proved false to him?" again interrupted Hatteras, in a hollow voice.

No one dared to look up, for the words weighed on them. The Doctor resumed his narrative, and said—

"The document I have mentioned gives the additional information of the death of Sir John Franklin. He sank under his fatigue on the 11th of June, 1847. Honor to his memory," he added, baring his head respectfully.

All the men silently followed his example. After a pause, Doctor Clawbonny went on to say—

H. M. S. *ships Erebus and Terror*

{ Wintered in the Ice in

28 of May 184 7 { Lat. 70° 5' N. Long. 98° 23' W

Having wintered in 1846—7 at Beechey Island
in Lat 74° 43' 28" N. Long 91° 39' 15" W after having
ascended Wellington Channel to Lat 77° and returned
by the West side of Cornwallis Island.

Sir John Franklin commanding the Expedition.

All well

Commander.

WHOEVER finds this paper is requested to forward it to the Secretary of
the Admiralty, London, *with a note of the time and place at which it was
found*: or, if more convenient, to deliver it for that purpose to the British
Consul at the nearest Port.

QUINCONQUE troùvera ce papier est prié d'y marquer le tems et lieu ou
il l'aura trouvé, et de le faire parvenir au plutot au Secrétaire de l'Amirauté
Britannique à Londres.

CUALQUIERA que hallare este Papel, se le suplica de enviarlo al Secretario
del Almirantazgo, en Londrés, con una nota del tiempo y del lugar en
donde se halló.

EEN ieder die dit Papier mogt vinden, wordt hiermede verzogt, om het
zelve, ten spoedigste, te willen zenden aan den Heer Minister van de
Marine der Nederlanden in 's Gravenhage, of wel aan den Secretaris der
Britsche Admiraliteit, te London, en daar by te voegen eene Nota,
inhoudende de tyd en de plaats alwaar dit Papier is gevonden geworden

FINDEREN af dette Papiir ombedes, naar Leiligbed gives, at sende
samme til Admiralitets Secretairen i London, eller nœrmeste Embedsmand
i Danmark, Norge, eller Sverrig. Tiden og Stœdit hvor dette er fundet
ønskes venskabeligt paategnet.

WER diesen Zettel findet, wird hier-durch ersucht denselben an den
Secretair des Admiralitets in London einzusenden, mit gefälliger angabe
an welchen ort und zu welcher zeit er gefundet worden ist.

Party consisting of 2 Officers and 6 Men
left the Ships on Monday 24th May 1847

Gm Gore Lieut

Chas F Des Voeux mate

"What became of the men after their admiral's death? Ten months elapsed before they forsook the ship, and the survivors then numbered one hundred and five men. Thirty-three were dead! A cairn was erected on Point Victory by order of the captains, Crozier and FitzJames, and in it this, their last document, was deposited. See, we are just passing the very place. You can still see the remains of this cairn on the very extremity of the point…and there is Erebus Bay, where they found the sloop made out of pieces of one of the ships and laid on a sled. They also discovered silver spoons there, tea and chocolate, besides religious books, and provisions in abundance. For the hundred and five survivors under the guidance of Captain Crozier set out for the Great Fish River. How far did they get? Did they reach Hudson's Bay? Do any of them still survive? Who can say what has become of them all now?"

"I can say what has become of them," replied John Hatteras, in loud, ringing tones. "Yes, they did reach Hudson's Bay, and divided into several parties. Yes, they took the route south, and in 1850 a letter of Dr. Rae mentioned the fact that on this very island before us the Eskimos fell in with a detachment of forty men hunting seals over the ice, dragging a boat with them, and looking pale and haggard, worn out with suffering and fatigue. And subsequently thirty corpses were found on the mainland, and five on an adjacent isle, some half buried, and some lying quite exposed; others under a boat turned upside down, and others still under the remains of a tent; here an officer, with his telescope on his shoulder and his loaded gun beside

The body of a sailor on the Franklin expedition was discovered in 1984, after almost 140 years in the Arctic ice.

him, and not far off cauldrons with the fragments of a ghastly sickening meal.

"On the receipt of this intelligence, the Admiralty requested the Hudson's Bay Company to dispatch experienced men to search the entire region. They explored the whole of the Back River to its mouth. They visited the islands of Montreal, Maconochie, and Point Ogle. But it was all in vain! Every one of the hapless company was dead! Dead from starvation, and pain and misery after making a horrible attempt to prolong their wretched lives by cannibalism! This is what has become of them! The route south is strewed with their mangled remains! Do you still desire to walk in their footsteps?"

Jules Verne
The English at the North Pole, 1875

Robert Peary Reaches the North Pole

The American Robert Peary claimed he had reached the North Pole on 6 April 1909. Peary's team was joined by seventeen Eskimos, nineteen sleds, and one hundred and thirty-three dogs, relying on Eskimo methods of survival.

During the daily march my mind and body were too busy with the problem of covering as many miles of distance as possible to permit me to enjoy the beauty of the frozen wilderness through which we tramped. But at the end of the day's march, while the igloos were being built, I usually had a few minutes in which to look about me and to realize the picturesqueness of our situation—we, the only living things in a trackless, colorless, inhospitable desert of ice. Nothing but the hostile ice, and far more hostile icy water, lay between our remote place on the world's map and the utmost tips of the lands of Mother Earth.

I knew of course that there was always a possibility that we might still end our lives up there, and that our conquest of the unknown spaces and silences of the polar void might remain forever unknown to the world that we had left behind. But it was hard to realize this. That hope which is said to spring eternal in the human breast always buoyed me up with the belief that, as a matter of course, we should be able to return along the white road by which we had come. Sometimes I would climb to the top of a pinnacle of ice to the north of our camp and strain my eyes into the whiteness that lay beyond, trying to imagine myself already at the Pole. We had come so far, and the capricious ice had placed so few obstructions in our path, that now I dared to loose my fancy, to entertain the image which my will had heretofore forbidden to my imagination— the image of ourselves at the goal....

We were now at the end of the last long march of the upward journey. Yet with the Pole actually in sight I was too weary to take the last few steps.

The accumulated weariness of all those days and nights of forced marches and insufficient sleep, constant peril, and anxiety, seemed to roll across me all at once. I was actually too exhausted to realize at the moment that my life's purpose had been achieved....

As there were indications that it [the sky] would clear before long, two of the Eskimos and myself made ready a light sled carrying only the instruments, a tin of pemmican, and one or two skins; and, drawn by a double team of dogs, we pushed on an estimated distance of ten miles. While we traveled, the sky cleared, and at the end of the journey, I was able to get a satisfactory series of observations at Columbia meridian midnight. These observations indicated that our position was then *beyond* the Pole. Nearly everything in the circumstances which then surrounded us seemed too strange to be thoroughly realized, but one of the strangest of those circumstances seemed to me to be the fact that, in a march of only a few hours, I had passed from the western to the eastern hemisphere and had verified my position at the summit of the world. It was hard to realize that, on the first miles of this brief march, we had been traveling precisely in the same direction.... Again, please consider the uncommon circumstance that, in order to return to our camp, it now became necessary to turn and go north again for a few miles and then to go directly south, all the time traveling in the same direction. As we passed back along that trail which none had ever seen before or would ever see again, certain reflections intruded themselves that, I think, may fairly be called unique. East, west, and north had disappeared for us. Only one direction remained, and that was south.

If it were possible for a man to arrive at 90° north latitude without being utterly exhausted, body and brain, he would doubtless enjoy a series of unique sensations and reflections. But the attainment of the Pole was the culmination of days and weeks of forced marches, physical discomfort, insufficient sleep, and racking anxiety. It is a wise provision of nature that the human consciousness can grasp only such degree of intense feeling as the brain can endure, and the grim guardians of earth's remotest spot will accept no man as guest until he has been tried and tested by the severest ordeal.

Robert F. Peary
The North Pole, 1910

Scott's Last Message

Cape Evans Base in Antarctica is dominated by a tall wooden cross. On the other side of the world, the British Museum in London displays Robert Falcon Scott's journal containing his last message to the British people, written before he died in March 1912.

The causes of the disaster are not due to faulty organisation, but to misfortune in all risks which had to be undertaken.

1. The loss of pony transport in March 1911 obliged me to start later than I had intended, and obliged the limits of stuff transported to be narrowed.

2. The weather throughout the outward journey, and especially the long gale in 83°S, stopped us.

3. The soft snow in lower reaches of glacier again reduced the pace.

We fought these untoward events with a will and conquered, but it cut into our provision reserve.

Every detail of our food supplies, clothing, and depots made on the interior ice-sheet and over that long stretch of 700 miles to the Pole and back, worked out to perfection. The advance party would have returned to the glacier in fine form and with a surplus of food, but for the astonishing failure of the man whom we had least expected to fail. Edgar Evans was thought the strongest man of the party.

The Beardmore Glacier is not difficult in fine weather, but on our return we did not get a single completely fine day; this with a sick companion enormously increased our anxieties.

As I have said elsewhere, we got into frightfully rough ice, and Edgar Evans received a concussion of the brain—he died a natural death, but left us a shaken party with the season unduly advanced.

But all the facts above enumerated were as nothing to the surprise which awaited us on the Barrier. I maintain that our arrangements for returning were quite adequate, and that no one in the world would have expected the temperatures and surfaces which we encountered at this time of the year. On the summit in lat. 85°/86° we had –20°, –30°. On the Barrier in lat. 82°, 10,000 feet lower, we had –30° in the day, –47° at night pretty regularly, with continuous headwind during our day marches. It is clear that these circumstances come on very suddenly, and our wreck is certainly due to this sudden advent of severe weather, which does not seem to have any satisfactory cause. I do not think human beings ever came through such a month as we have come through, and we should have got through in spite of the weather but for the sickening of a second companion, Captain Oates, and a shortage of fuel in our depots for which I cannot account, and finally, but for the storm which has fallen on us within 11 miles of the depot at which we hoped to secure our final supplies. Surely misfortune could scarcely have exceeded this last blow. We arrived within 11 miles of our old One Ton Camp with fuel for one hot meal and food for two days. For four days we have been unable to leave the tent—the gale howling about us. We are

In Respectful Memory of
THE GREAT HERO
Captain R. SCOTT, R.N.
AND HIS NOBLE COMPANIONS,
who succumbed in their endeavours for
Scientific Research in the Antarctic.
The last and greatest Expedition.
GONE BUT NOT FORGOTTEN

weak, writing is difficult, but for my own sake I do not regret this journey, which has shown that Englishmen can endure hardships, help one another, and meet death with as great a fortitude as ever in the past.

We took risks, we knew we took them; things have come out against us, and therefore we have no cause for complaint, but bow to the will of Providence, determined still to do our best to the last....

Had we lived, I should have had a tale to tell of the hardihood, endurance, and courage of my companions which would have stirred the heart of every Englishman. These rough notes and our dead bodies must tell the tale, but surely, surely, a great rich country like ours will see that those who are dependent on us are properly provided for.

Robert Falcon Scott

Shackleton's Epic Voyage

Ernest Shackleton obtained a substantial loan from a group of businessmen for his voyage to the South Pole, pledging the receipts from sales of the expedition photographs as a guarantee. When the Endurance *was wrecked, the negatives lay several feet under water. Frank Hurley, the expedition photographer, dived in to recover them, and they are now in Cambridge, England.*

On his return from the Antarctic Shackleton gave lectures to pay his debts.

These men dressed as bears (an animal unknown in the Antarctic) are advertising a movie of his journey.

Open pack ice with many channels (top). The *Endurance* (above) cuts a trail through young ice.

There are no channels in the ice pack. In the foreground are pressure ridges in the ice.

F rank Worsley (above) observes the altitude of a star with a theodolite.

T he expedition team photograph (above left): Shackleton is in the first row, third from the left.

T he living quarters of the *Endurance* (far left), which all on board referred to as "the Ritz."

T he dogs (left) were housed in igloos on the ice.

October 1915

"Shackleton said: 'This is the end of the poor old ship. She's done for. We shall have to abandon her, as I warned you.' I made no answer but looked at her timber ends, which had opened out and let the water pour, like a cataract, into the ship."

Frank Worsley
Endurance, 1931

24 April 1916

With a rousing cheer we slid the *James Caird* down the gravelly beach and launched her through the surf....

Frank Hurley (left), the twenty-eight-year-old expedition photographer. Australian by birth, he had already wintered at Cape Denison with Douglas Mawson.

For six months the twenty-eight men (top) lived on a raft of ice drifting gently north.

Frank Hurley and Sir Ernest Shackleton (above) in front of their tent. The stove ran on seal blubber.

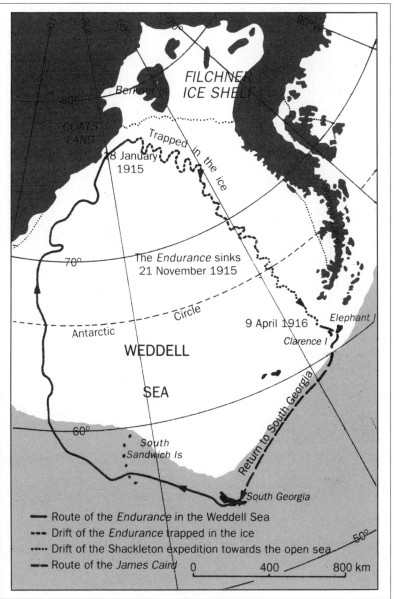

FILCHNER ICE SHELF

Berkner Is

COATS LAND

Trapped in the ice

8 January 1915

The *Endurance* sinks
21 November 1915

Antarctic Circle

9 April 1916   Elephant I

Clarence I

WEDDELL

SEA

Return to South Georgia

South Sandwich Is

South Georgia

— Route of the *Endurance* in the Weddell Sea
--- Drift of the *Endurance* trapped in the ice
····· Drift of the Shackleton expedition towards the open sea
–– Route of the *James Caird*

0   400   800 km

Before Shackleton and his gallant companions lay a voyage of 750 miles, across the most tempestuous ocean in the world....

James Francis Hurley
Shackleton's Argonauts
1948

Again and again we discussed the best point to make for....

"What do you think about Cape Horn?" he [Shackleton] asked, adding, "it's the nearest."

"Yes," I replied, "but we can never reach it. The westerly gales would blow us away. With luck, though, we might fetch the Falkland Islands."

"I am afraid that, although it is the longest run," he remarked, "we shall have to make for South Georgia, as you originally suggested. The gales will drive us to leeward...."

"We've had some great adventures together, Skipper," he said suddenly: "but this is the greatest of all. This time it really is do or die, as they say in the story-books."

Frank Worsley, *Endurance*
1931

The running gear would not work, and the flag was frozen into a solid mass, so he tied his jersey to the top of the pole for a signal. Wild put a pick through our last remaining tin of petrol, and, soaking coats, mitts, and socks with it, carried them to the top of Penguin Hill, and soon they were ablaze. Suddenly [the *Yelcho*] stopped, a boat was lowered, and we could recognize Sir Ernest's figure as he climbed down the ladder....

"Thank God the Boss is safe."

Ernest Shackleton, *South*
1919

Wally Herbert's Journey Across the Top of the World

On 21 February 1968 the British explorer Wally Herbert set out with three companions, four sleds, and forty huskies from Point Barrow, Alaska. Over a year later, on 6 April 1969, he became the first man to reach the North Pole with dogsleds.

At 0200 hours Greenwich mean time on 6th April 1969, my three companions and I reached the North Pole, and by so doing became the first surface travelers whose claim to have reached that elusive point has never been contested. Less controversially, we were the first *British* expedition to reach the North Pole; the first, and still the *only* men to arrive there on foot by the longest route from Point Barrow in Alaska via the so-called Pole of Inaccessibility, and the first, and still the *only* pedestrians who, having reached the North Pole (or its general vicinity), did not thereupon retrace our footsteps or call in an aircraft to lift us out.

Our plan was unique in this respect—a one-way journey across the pack ice of the Arctic Ocean—a journey based on the nagging uncertainty of the calculated risk. There were no points of contact along the way, no exit routes, no chance of escape, no honorable way of ending the ordeal except by completing the course. It was a journey inspired by a love of history. A journey urged on through those moments of fear by the even greater fear of embarrassment, and the shame of failure.

For us, then, our point of no return was the first step of a hazardous trek taking sixteen months to complete —a journey of 3800 miles across pack ice in a constant state of motion and deformation as the winds and currents churned it around, fracturing it and pressuring it and grinding it into mush ice which would not bear the weight of man. Across this, the most unstable surface on the face of Earth, we planned to make a journey that could not possibly be upstaged by some

Wally Herbert (on the left) and his team at the North Pole.

future expedition, and one that was most unlikely ever to repeated, for our competitive spirit and, I am proud to admit it, our sense of patriotic duty would settle for nothing less than the first surface crossing of the Arctic Ocean—and by its *longest* axis....

On 23rd February [1969], the floe split up, and we were forced to abandon our hut and begin the second year of our journey. At the time we were 322 miles from the North Pole. It was dark; it was cold, and the ice was very broken up. We were at this time burning up 7500 calories a day, and the dogs and men would sometimes leave vapor trails so thick that the following teams would have to cut new tracks in order to see the way. And slowly, painfully slowly, we closed in on the Pole.

Traveling for ten hours a day in temperatures down to minus 45°C [–49°F], there seemed no end to the misery; but at our lowest ebb the sun returned and, for the first time in five months, that beautiful, pulsating, living thing seemed slowly to explode itself out of the sea.

Then once again the mists rolled in, and as they thickened as we neared the Pole, the sun shone through them without warmth or light enough to cast a shadow. Day and night now fused together—we had reached that point on the surface of the Earth where all directions are south.

We went onto a forced march routine and for fifteen hours a day and every day we forced the pace in a desperate bid to reach Spitsbergen before the break-up of the ice—and

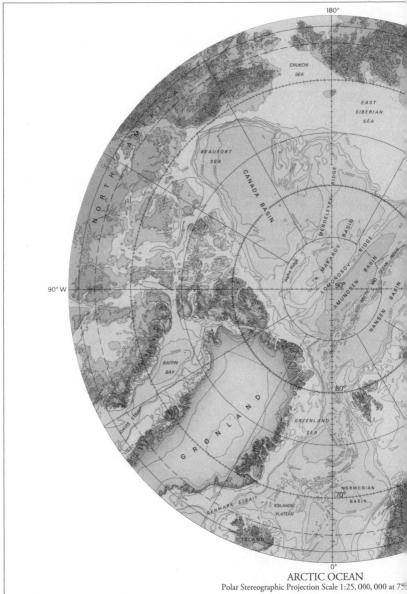

ARCTIC OCEAN
Polar Stereographic Projection Scale 1:25, 000, 000 at 75°

there were many times in this stage of the journey when we came within a hair's breadth of losing the one thing we still had in our favor—the element of luck....

Several times that day [23 May] we searched the horizon, but without success. Then at 10:50 P.M. I noticed a large hummock past which the other three sleds had swept without stopping, and climbing this hummock I stuck a harpoon into its summit, steadied my rifle against it, and took aim at the cloud base directly ahead. Through the telescopic sight I suddenly saw land—it was climbing out of the horizon into the cloud rolls; a gray and white wall of land, hazy with distance, hostile-looking, bleak, and spanning several degrees. I lowered my aim very slightly to the pack ice—now I could see all three sleds in line ahead, widely separated, but dead on course.

During the next six days we waded through slush and meltwater up to our shins and hacked our way through some of the most chaotic ice we had ever seen. We were constantly harassed by bears, and it was becoming depressingly obvious that our chances of making a landing were decreasing by the hour and that the last few miles were going to be the most hazardous few miles of the entire journey. Finally, after several attempts...a landing was made on a small rocky island—thus concluding the first surface crossing of the Arctic Ocean. The date was 29th May 1969.

Wally Herbert
"The First Surface Crossing of the Arctic Ocean"
Pole Nord 1983
1987

John Ross and the Eskimos

There was little to do on board ship during the long Arctic winter, and visits from the Eskimos provided welcome distraction. Englishman John Ross tells of his encounters with them in the diaries he kept on his expedition in search of the Northwest Passage in 1818.

August 10. About ten o'clock this day, we were rejoiced to see eight sleds, driven by the natives, advancing by a circuitous route towards the place where we lay; they halted about a mile from us, and the people, alighting, ascended a small iceberg, as if to reconnoiter. After remaining apparently in consultation for nearly half an hour, four of them descended and came towards the flagstaff, which, however, they did not venture to approach. In the meantime a white flag was hoisted at the main in each ship, and John Sacheuse dispatched, bearing a small white flag, with some presents, that he might endeavor, if possible, to bring them to a parley.

First communication with the natives of Prince Regent Bay.

This was a service for which he had most cheerfully volunteered, requesting leave to go unattended and unarmed, a request to which no objection could be made as the place chosen for the meeting was within half a mile of the *Isabella.* It was equally advantageous to the natives, a canal, or small chasm in the ice, not passable without a plank, separating the parties from each other, and preventing any possibility of an attack from these people, unless by darts.

In exacting this service, Sacheuse displayed no less address than courage. Having placed his flag at some distance from the canal, he advanced to the edge and, taking off his hat, made friendly signs for those opposite to approach, as he did; this they partly complied with, halting at a distance of three hundred yards, where they got out of their sleds and set up a loud simultaneous halloo, which Sacheuse answered by imitating it. They ventured to approach a little nearer, having nothing in their hands but the whips with which they guide their dogs; and, after satisfying themselves that the canal was impassable, one of them in particular seemed to acquire confidence. Shouts, words, and gestures were exchanged for some time to no purpose, though each party seemed, in some degree, to recognize each other's language. Sacheuse, after a time, thought he could discover that they spoke the Humooke dialect, drawing out their words, however, to an unusual length. He immediately adopted their dialect and, holding up the presents, called out to them, "*Kahkeiten* [Come on]!" to which they answered, "*Naakrie, naakrieai-plaite* [No, no—go away]"; and other words which he made out to mean that they hoped we were not come to destroy them.

The boldest then approached the edge of the canal, and, drawing from his boot a knife, repeated, "Go away; I can kill you." Sacheuse, not intimidated, told them he was also a man and a friend, and, at the same time, threw across the canal some strings of beads and a chequed shirt, but these they beheld with great distrust and apprehension, still calling "Go away, don't kill us." Sacheuse now threw them an English knife, saying "Take that." On this they approached with caution, picked up the knife, then shouted and pulled their noses; these actions were imitated by Sacheuse, who, in return, called out, "Heigh, yaw!" pulling his nose with the same gesture. They now pointed to the shirt, demanding what it was and, when told it was an article of clothing, asked of what skin it was made. Sacheuse replied, it was made of the hair of an animal that they had never seen; on which they picked it up with expressions of surprise.

They now began to ask many questions; for, by this time, they found the language spoken by them-selves and Sacheuse had sufficient resemblance to enable them to hold some communication.

They first pointed to the ships, eagerly asking, "What great creatures are those?" "Do they come from the sun or the moon?" "Do they give us light by night or by day?" Sacheuse told them that he was a man, that he had a father and mother like themselves; and, pointing to the south, said that he came from a distant country in that direction. To this they answered, "That cannot be, there is nothing but ice there." They again asked "What creatures are these?" pointing to the ships; to which Sacheuse replied that "they are houses made of wood." This they seemed still to discredit, answering, "No, they are alive, we have seen them move their wings." Sacheuse now inquired of them what they themselves were; to which they replied, they were men, and lived in that direction, pointing to the north; that there was much water there; and that they had come here to fish for sea unicorns. It was then agreed that Sacheuse should cross over the chasm to them, and he accordingly returned to the ship to make his report and to ask for a plank.

During the whole of this conversation I had been employed, with a good telescope, in observing their motions; and beheld the first man approach with every mark of fear and distrust, looking frequently behind to the other two, and beckoning them to come on, as if for support. They occasionally retreated, then advanced again, with cautious steps, in the attitude of listening, generally keeping one hand down by their knees, in readiness to pull out a knife which they had in their boots...

John Ross

Officers visit a village of igloos (above), while a pair of Eskimos invited aboard the *Victory* (below) try to draw a map of the area.

Arctic Wildlife

In the air, on the ice, in the water, or on the tundra: the Arctic teems with life.

The musk ox, an endangered species, inhabits the tundra.

The polar bear, found only in the northern hemisphere, is the king of the ice: a carnivore of 750 pounds, its preferred prey is the seal. Eskimos hunt the bear for its fur and fat.

The walrus—which can weigh as much as 3300 pounds—uses its tusks to probe in search of food and to move across the ice.

The seal is heavily hunted for its blubber and skin by Eskimos.

Penguins at the South Pole

A surprising number of animal species live in the Antarctic, despite the inhospitable environment. The most curious are the penguins, birds that do not fly but can swim adeptly.

Two of the penguin species found in Antarctica: the Adélie (below and opposite top) and the emperor (right).

Emperor penguins lay their eggs in the middle of winter. The males incubate the eggs, keeping them warm under a fold in their abdomen. The chick spends its first weeks with one of its parents, protected from the cold by thick down.

Emperor penguins live in huge colonies, the largest numbering some 50,000.

Northern Sea Route

While the Northwest Passage remains largely unused, the Northeast Passage, renamed the Northern Sea Route by the Soviets, is now of considerable economic and political importance, having benefited from substantial investment.

Thousands of specialists oversee the running of the Northern Sea Route, which is equipped with ports, airfields, and weather stations servicing the largest fleet of polar freighter and icebreakers in the world.

The year 1932 was a landmark: the *Sibiriakov* navigated the Northern Sea Route in two months and earned the congratulations of Joseph Stalin, who soon made the following decree:

"1. [That] in the Council of People's Commissars of the U.S.S.R. be organized a Central Administration of the Northern Sea Route (GUSMP). [That] the GUSMP be charged with final development of the Northern Sea Route from the White Sea to the Bering Strait, including full equipment of this route, maintenance of it, and procurement of means for the safety of navigation over the same.

2. [That] to the GUSMP be transferred all existing meteorological and radio stations located on the coast and islands in the Arctic."

The man who had recently made the crossing in the *Sibiriakov*, Otto Schmidt, was put in charge of GUSMP, and his authority was later extended to cover the whole economic development of northern Siberia, in particular the Arctic ports and the geological and mining sectors.

International cargo can be transported on special freighters escorted by Soviet icebreakers along the Northern Sea Route.

Maritime traffic developed first in the west in the Kara Sea, starting from the Ob and Yenisey Rivers, but also in the east from the Lena and Kolyma Rivers to the Bering Strait. The 100 to 300,000 tons annually carried through these waters before World War II have increased to an estimated 4,000,000 tons.

In August 1977 the Soviets astonished the world by announcing that the *Arktika* had reached the North Pole. It was the first vessel to do this on the surface of the sea, achieving an average speed on its voyage there and back of 11.5 knots. In 1978 the icebreaker *Sibir* escorted a freighter along a route north of Novaya Zemlya and the New Siberian Islands. However, though these powerful nuclear icebreakers were able to go virtually everywhere, many vessels, particularly freighters, have experienced difficulties from the pressure of ice in the region—it remains difficult to predict the state of the ice pack. Indeed in October 1983, at the end of the season, 51 ships were frozen in north of Pevek, some 550 miles west of the Bering Strait. Three nuclear icebreakers hastened to the area and worked for one month to free the ships, only one of which sank, though 30 were damaged. A program to build more powerful ships has begun and will doubtless one day achieve an even more direct transarctic passage, more than 700 miles shorter than the coastal route.

Information from Terence Armstrong

Icebreakers

Icebreakers and ice-strengthened freighters are the current vehicles of ocean and river transport in the Arctic. The Soviet Union has the largest fleet in the world: eighteen icebreakers and some three hundred ice-strengthened freighters. The next largest fleets are owned by the United States and Canada.

Launched in 1898, the 10,000-horsepower *Yermak* (below left) was the first Russian icebreaker. It remained in service until 1963.

The *Polar Star* and the *Polar Sea* (right) are modern American icebreakers. Built in 1973 and 1975, they are 400 feet long and have a crew of 125, plus 13 officers.

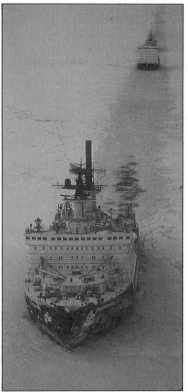

The Soviet nuclear icebreaker *Sibir* (75,000 horsepower) opens a channel in the ice pack (right) for a polar freighter in the Northern Sea Route.

The finest of the European polar ships, the *Polarstern* (below), belongs to the Alfred Wegener Institute in Hamburg. It is used for research in the Arctic and Antarctic.

Antarctica Ice

Until 1955 virtually nothing was known about the Antarctic ice cap. The volume of ice represents nearly 70 percent of the fresh water on the earth. Multinational projects are now studying the glacial features of the region.

Analysis of deep ice cores and the impurities trapped therein makes it possible to trace the evolution of our atmosphere.

The layers deposited over the last hundred years, for example, give evidence of volcanic eruptions, cosmic happenings, and nuclear fall-out. The full extent of the pollution caused by human activity is also revealed by the carbon dioxide content of the preindustrial atmosphere conserved in the ice.

Drilling at greater depth makes it possible to identify different climatic stages. During the ice age—at its height some 18,000 years ago—temperatures were significantly lower in comparison to the warmer climate the earth has experienced in the past 10,000 years. The present glacial period is characterized by dangerous modifications in our environment: a significantly higher content of carbon dioxide and a substantial increase in aerosols. The ice cap has by contrast remained relatively stable during the deglaciation.

The Dynamics of Ice

By the force of gravity successive layers of snow sink onto the ice cap and turn to ice while becoming thinner and creeping towards the coast. Precipitation is thus progressively discharged into the sea.

During the International Geophysical Year (1957–8) the movement

The Frenchman Claude Lorius, former president of the Scientific Committee for Antarctic Research (left), photographed at the Soviet Antarctic base, Vostok, studying ice samples on an international glaciological project.

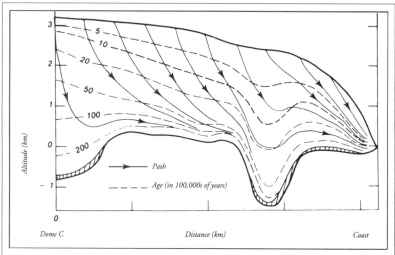

The path of the ice is calculated by simulating its movement between a point identified as Dome C at 3000 m altitude, 1200 km from the coast, and the Dumont d'Urville Base.

of the coastal glaciers was determined by geodesic methods, using rocky protuberances as reference points. The launching of geodesic satellites made it possible to measure the rates of movement (by the Doppler principle) in the central regions of Antarctica, where they are very low—about three feet per year—progressively increasing to an average of 300 feet per year on the peripheries.

The most active glaciers and shelves advance 1–2 miles a year. An immense quantity of ice is released during this process—mainly in the form of icebergs. Nearly half of the ice comes from three shelves (Amery, Filchner, and Ross).

There is not yet enough data to show an imbalance in the loss and gain of the mass of the ice cap; but infor-mation about the surface contours, the rocky substratum, and the quantity of the accumulated snow serves to construct models of the discharge from the inland ice sheet.

A Historical Record of Our Atmosphere

It was in the International Geophysical Year that the collection and study of deep ice cores began, made possible by the development of boring techniques and sophisticated methods of laboratory analysis. The cores are used to study the transformation of snow into névé and then ice (the latter is found some hundreds of feet deep in the central regions, with a density of some 0.82) and also to study the plastic properties of the substance.

Knowledge of the composition of the

ice and its associated impurities over the ages provides a unique historical record of the evolution of the climate and the impact of human activity on the atmosphere. These are subjects with a direct bearing on the environmental problems of today.

During the last 1.7 million years the climate of the earth has oscillated between ice ages (characterized particularly by the formation of huge ice sheets on the continents of the northern hemisphere and a fall in the sea level of over 300 feet) and warmer periods, of much shorter duration, such as that in which we now live. The composition of the atmosphere has been significantly disturbed by emissions, particularly of carbon dioxide, caused by human activity.

The atmosphere is now monitored, but the observations date back no more than twenty years at best. Only the glacial records make it possible to reconstruct the climate and chemical composition of the atmosphere over a time scale that gives a proper perspective and shows the important factors and mechanisms at work. The information obtained, whether it relates to the beginning of the industrial age or to very different climatic conditions (for example the last ice age), is moreover needed to construct models of the climate, which may in due course provide a means of forecasting.

Sampling Techniques

While it is easy to take samples of layers deposited in recent decades (from holes driven up to 30 feet deep), increasingly unwieldy equipment is needed to reach greater depths. Up to 300 feet (which can represent some 1000 years), the sample is taken by successive extractions with a rotating drill fitted with blades or a tube equipped at the tip with a heating element to melt the ice. The gathering of samples becomes more laborious as the depth increases; apart from the difficulty of recovering the totality of the extracts or the outwash (thus avoiding blocking the core barrel), the hole is liable to be closed by deformation of the ice. Penetration then becomes impossible, and, at a depth of 3000 feet (where one finds the deposits of the last ice age, some 20,000 years ago), specialized drilling fluid has to be supplied, involving increasingly complicated equipment. Some tens of tons of material have typically to be transported to take a bore of this kind, as has been done at the American station Byrd, by the Soviets at Vostok, and by a French team at Dome C.

Claude Lorius
Review of the Palace of Discovery
April 1984

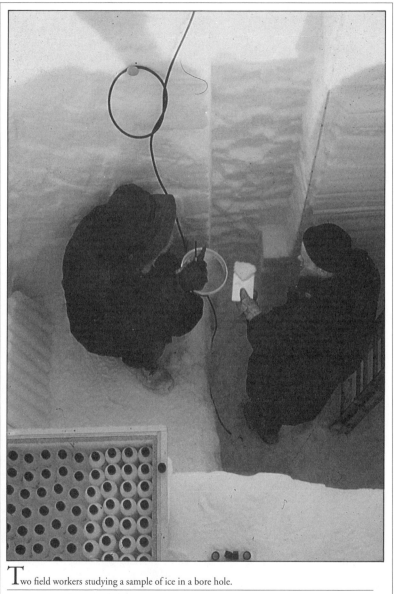

Two field workers studying a sample of ice in a bore hole.

Antarctica Today

Since 1959 the status of Antarctica has been defined by an international treaty holding all national claims in abeyance and laying the ground for the signatory nations to pursue the research of the International Geophysical Year in a spirit of cooperation.

The Antarctic Treaty

The Governments of Argentina, Australia, Belgium, Chile, the French Republic, Japan, New Zealand, Norway, the Union of South Africa, the Union of Soviet Socialist Republics, the United Kingdom of Great Britain and Northern Ireland, and the United States of America;

Recognizing that it is in the interest of all mankind that Antarctica shall continue forever to be used exclusively for peaceful purposes and shall not become the scene or object of international discord;

Acknowledging the substantial contributions to scientific knowledge resulting from international cooperation in scientific investigation in Antarctica;

Convinced that the establishment of a firm foundation for the continuation and development of such cooperation on the basis of freedom of scientific investigation in Antarctica as applied during the International Geophysical Year accords with the interests of science and the progress of all mankind;

Convinced also that a treaty ensuring the use of Antarctica for peaceful purposes only and the continuance of international harmony in Antarctica will further the purposes and principles embodied in the Charter of the United Nations;

Have agreed as follows:

ARTICLE I—
1. Antarctica shall be used for peaceful purposes only. There shall be prohibited, *inter alia*, any measures of a military nature, such as the establishment of military bases and fortifications, the carrying out of

military maneuvers, as well as the testing of any type of weapons.

2. The present Treaty shall not prevent the use of military personnel or equipment for scientific research or for any other peaceful purpose.

ARTICLE II—Freedom of scientific investigation in Antarctica and co-operation toward that end, as applied during the International Geophysical Year, shall continue, subject to the provisions of the present Treaty.

ARTICLE III—

1. In order to promote international cooperation in scientific investigation in Antarctica, as provided for in Article II of the present Treaty, the Contracting Parties agree that, to the greatest extent feasible and practicable:

(a) Information regarding plans for scientific programs in Antarctica shall be exchanged to permit maximum economy and efficiency of operations;

(b) Scientific personnel shall be exchanged in Antarctica between expeditions and stations;

(c) Scientific observations and results from Antarctica shall be exchanged and made freely available.

2. In implementing this Article, every encouragement shall be given to the establishment of cooperative working relations with those specialized agencies of the United Nations and other international organizations having a scientific or technical interest in Antarctica.

ARTICLE IV—

1. Nothing contained in the present Treaty shall be interpreted as:

(a) A renunciation by any Contracting Party of previously asserted rights of or claims to territorial sovereignty in Antarctica;

(b) A renunciation or diminution by any Contracting Party of any basis of claim to territorial sovereignty in Antarctica which it may have whether as a result of its activities or those of its nationals in Antarctica, or otherwise;

(c) Prejudicing the position of any Contracting Party as regards its recognition or nonrecognition of any other State's right of or claim or basis of claim to territorial sovereignty in Antarctica.

2. No acts or activities taking place while the present Treaty is in force shall constitute a basis for asserting, supporting, or denying a claim to territorial sovereignty in Antarctica or create any rights of sovereignty in Antarctica. No new claim, or enlargement of an existing claim, to territorial sovereignty in Antarctica shall be asserted while the present Treaty is in force.

ARTICLE V—

1. Any nuclear explosions in Antarctica and the disposal there of radioactive waste material shall be prohibited.

2. In the event of the conclusion of international agreements concerning the use of nuclear energy, including nuclear explosions and the disposal of radioactive waste material, to which all of the Contracting Parties whose representatives are entitled to participate in the meetings provided for under Article IX are parties, the rules established under such agreements shall apply in Antarctica.

ARTICLE VI—The provisions of the present Treaty shall apply to the area south of 60° South Latitude, including all ice shelves, but nothing in the present Treaty shall prejudice or in any way affect the rights, or the exercise of the rights, of any State under international law with regard to the high seas within that area.

[Articles VII-XIII lay down the terms under which the Treaty will be enforced.]

ARTICLE XIV—The present Treaty, done in the English, French, Russian, and Spanish languages, each version being equally authentic, shall be deposited in the archives of the Government of the United States of America, which shall transmit duly certified copies thereof to the Governments of the signatory and acceding States.

In Witness Whereof, the undersigned Plenipotentiaries, duly authorized, have signed the present Treaty.

Done at Washington this first day of December one thousand nine hundred and fifty-nine.

[By 1991 the Treaty had been signed by 39 countries.]

Organization of Research in Antarctica Today

Some 1500 people winter in Antarctica to do research, and the population noticeably rises in the summer season. There are now (1991) 49 permanent stations run by 17 countries; 29 are on the continent, which is the size of Europe and the United States combined, and 20 in the Antarctic islands. Among the more recent countries to take part are Germany, India, Poland, and China.

In keeping with the spirit of the International Geophysical Year, and in the interests of efficiency, the various research programs are coordinated by an international committee, SCAR (Scientific Committee for Antarctic Research), presently comprising 24 member states and 4 associates. The Committee is not empowered to make decisions but plays an important part organizing working groups and symposia and planning Antarctic contributions to global programs.

The United States had by far the largest program in the International Geophysical Year (1957–8). The department of the National Science Foundation responsible for polar projects now runs three Antarctic stations: Palmer in the Antarctic peninsula, the Amundsen-Scott Base at the South Pole, and the main base, McMurdo, where the population reaches 800 in the summer.

An icebreaker escorts the yearly passage of a freighter and a tanker across the ocean, while the personnel and part of the equipment arrive by airplane from Christchurch, New Zealand. At the beginning of the Antarctic spring the Americans use large transport aircraft with landing wheels, C141s, and ski-equipped Hercules. There is a landing strip at McMurdo on the Ross Ice Shelf and another on the sea ice. By the end of November the state of the ice precludes the use of aircraft with landing wheels, and only the Hercules continue to fly until February.

The USSR founded the Arctic and Antarctic Institute in St. Petersburg. It runs six bases, of which the most important, Molodezhnaya, alone numbers up to 150 winter residents.

A fleet comprising two tankers, one or two research ships and five

Aerial view of the British base, Rothera, and the new gravel airstrip.

freighters, all designed for navigation in the ice, gather each summer in Antarctic waters. The Soviets have for some years operated a direct flight between St. Petersburg and Molodezhnaya via Aden and Maputo in Mozambique.

In France Antarctic operations depend on the ministries of overseas territories and research and technology, rather than the ministries responsible for research, as is the case in Britain, Germany, and the United States. The TAAF (Terres Australes et Antarctiques Françaises)

runs several stations in the islands of the peri-Antarctic, notably at Kerguelen, and the Dumont d'Urville observatory in Terre Adélie, and also participates in multinational Antarctic projects.

In Britain the government's research is undertaken by the British Antarctic Survey. Formerly the Falkland Islands Dependencies Survey, it has since 1967 been part of the Natural Environment Research Council. The British run three geophysical observatories on the continent and three biological and one

The entrance of the American Amundsen-Scott Base at the geographic South Pole.

meteorological station in the Antarctic islands. The main station is Halley, above which the thinning of the ozone layer was first discovered. It was set up by the Royal Society during the International Geophysical Year on the nearly 500-foot-thick Brunt Ice Shelf and has been rebuilt five times (stations in the Antarctic are liable to be progressively buried by snow).

Supplies are brought annually by two Royal Research Ships, the *Bransfield* and the *James Clark Ross*. The latter, launched in 1990, can accommodate 50 research workers and a crew of 27. Both ships are equipped to receive satellite images of weather conditions and sea ice coverage. The BAS Air Unit operates four de

Havilland wheel-ski Twin Otter Aircraft and one Dash 7 type aircraft from a recently built airstrip at Rothera Base.

West Germany has been an important and relatively new presence in the Antarctic. In 1980 the Ministry of Research and Technology founded the Alfred Wegener Institute in Bremershaven for the purpose of Arctic and Antarctic research. A year later the Institute opened the G. von Neumayer base on the Antarctic continent at the eastern entrance to the Weddell Sea. In 1982 Germany brought into commission a magnificent ice-strengthened ship of 11,000 tons powered by 20,000-horsepower engines, the *Polarstern*, equipped with cabins and laboratories to accommodate a hundred people.

Important oceanographic work is being undertaken in the Weddell Sea in collaboration with other countries under the direction of Professor Hempel. A German team (which has become multinational) has been studying the glaciology of the Filchner-Ronne Ice Shelf at the head of the Weddell Sea. Like the Ross Ice Shelf this is a vast sheet of ice almost the size of France and several hundred yards deep. It has a determining part to play in the continued existence—or future disappearance—of the western Antarctic inland ice sheet.

The Japanese established themselves in Antarctica in the International Geophysical Year, building the base of Syowa, which is about 130 miles west of Molodezhnaya. They now run two bases there.

In 1965 they brought into commission a 5000-ton ice-strengthened ship, the *Fuji*, equipped to resupply their base in a zone of difficult access and also carry out oceanographic work. The *Fuji* was replaced in 1982 by the *Shirase*. This 12,000-ton ship, with engines of 30,000 horsepower, is as powerful as today's American icebreakers.

From 1968 to 1969 the Japanese made a particularly difficult expedition from the base of Syowa to the South Pole and back, a distance of 3224 miles over a little-known part of the continent where the altitude rises to 12,139 feet. Special snow vehicles were built specifically for the project. Geophysicists and glaciologists lived and worked in them for the duration, a period of 141 days.

Of all the 49 stations now main-tained south of the 60th parallel only two are in the interior of the continent: the American Amundsen-Scott Base and the Soviet Vostok Base. On King George Island in the South Shetlands, in contrast, eight countries operate eight stations in unfortunate proximity to each other, only a few miles apart.

Outside the government expeditions, which are dedicated to research, no industrial activity is at present carried on in Antarctica, with the obvious exception of fishing. The catch includes krill, a tiny shrimp-like creature found in abundance. Whaling has been controlled after the excesses of the past hundred years.

Under the Antarctic Treaty measures have been taken to conserve the marine living resources and flora and fauna of the region, all of which are vulnerable to the incursions of humans. In an area where less than two percent of the land is free of ice, human activity is a particularly serious threat to animal breeding grounds.

Pollution and waste disposal also pose special problems: buried matter, rather than rotting away, is preserved in the freezing temperatures; and loose rubbish is scattered far and wide in what is the windiest place in the world. It is now policy to transport everything apart from human and kitchen waste elsewhere for disposal.

The major issue in 1991 was the draft proposal to ban oil and mineral exploitation for at least fifty years. It was eventually supported by all thirty-nine signatories to the Treaty.

Bertrand Imbert
Information from
the Scott Polar Research Institute
and the British Antarctic Survey

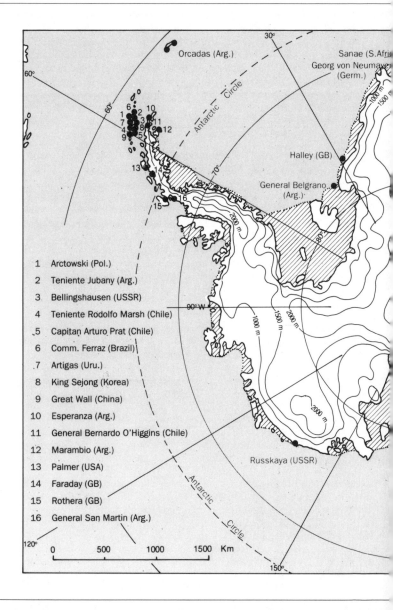

1 Arctowski (Pol.)
2 Teniente Jubany (Arg.)
3 Bellingshausen (USSR)
4 Teniente Rodolfo Marsh (Chile)
5 Capitan Arturo Prat (Chile)
6 Comm. Ferraz (Brazil)
7 Artigas (Uru.)
8 King Sejong (Korea)
9 Great Wall (China)
10 Esperanza (Arg.)
11 General Bernardo O'Higgins (Chile)
12 Marambio (Arg.)
13 Palmer (USA)
14 Faraday (GB)
15 Rothera (GB)
16 General San Martin (Arg.)

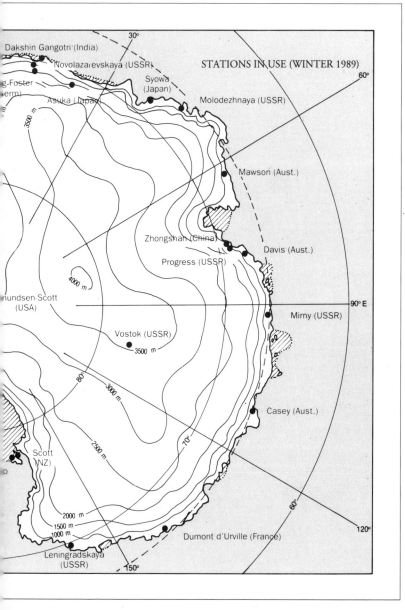

STATIONS IN USE (WINTER 1989)

Dakshin Gangotri (India)
Novolazarevskaya (USSR)
g-Foster
erm)
Asuka (Japan)
Syowa (Japan)
Molodezhnaya (USSR)
Mawson (Aust.)
Zhongshan (China)
Davis (Aust.)
Progress (USSR)
undsen-Scott (USA)
Mirny (USSR)
Vostok (USSR)
3500 m
Casey (Aust.)
Scott (NZ)
3500 m
4000 m
3000 m
2500 m
2000 m
1500 m
1000 m
Dumont d'Urville (France)
Leningradskaya (USSR)
30°
60°
90° E
120°
150°
80°
70°
60°

Arctic	Antarctic
330 B.C. Pytheas, a Greek navigator of Massilia (Marseilles), probably reaches Iceland **983** Erik the Red founds a Norwegian colony in Greenland	
	1405–33 Admiral Cheng Ho leads six expeditions with numerous junks in the Indian Ocean and along the coast of Africa (China) **1497** Vasco da Gama rounds the Cape of Good Hope (Portugal) **1520** Magellan discovers the Strait of Magellan, then sails to the Philippines (Spain)
1553 Sir Hugh Willoughby and his commander, Chancellor, sail in search of the Northeast Passage (Great Britain) **1576–8** Martin Frobisher makes three voyages in search of the Northwest Passage (GB) **1585–7** John Davis makes three voyages in search of the Northwest Passage (GB) **1594–7** William Barents makes three voyages in search of the Northeast Passage (Holland) **1609–11** Henry Hudson makes two voyages in search of the Northwest Passage. Discovers Hudson Bay (GB)	
1648 Semyon Dezhnev navigates the passage between Siberia and Alaska (Russia) **1721** The pastor Hans Egede colonizes Greenland and propagates the gospel (Denmark and Norway) **1725–42** Vitus Bering, then the Great Northern Expedition, explores the Bering Strait and the whole north coast of Siberia (Russia)	**1616** Le Maire and Schouten round Cape Horn (Holland) **1642** Abel Tasman discovers Van Diemen's Land (Tasmania) and the west coast of New Zealand, which he takes to be the northern shore of Antarctica (Holland)
	1739 Bouvet discovers the island named after him in the South Atlantic (France) **1773** James Cook crosses the Antarctic Circle with the *Resolution* and the *Adventure* (GB)
1778 James Cook explores the coast of Alaska and northeast Siberia (GB)	
1818 John Ross searches for the Northwest Passage in vain (GB)	**1819** William Smith discovers the South Shetlands aboard the *Williams* (GB)
1819–20 Edward Parry on the *Hecla* and the *Griper* discovers part of the Northwest Passage, as far as Melville Island (GB)	**1819–20** Edward Bransfield sights the Antarctic peninsula aboard the *Williams* (GB) Fabian Bellingshausen circumnavigates the Antarctic on the *Vostok* and the *Mirny* (Russia)
1819–22 John Franklin discovers the other half of the Northwest Passage overland (GB) **1820–3** Ferdinand von Wrangel explores the length of the Siberian coast between Kolyma and Cape Dezhnev with dogsleds and sights the island named after him (Russia)	**1821–2** The sealers Benjamin Pendleton and Nathaniel Palmer discover the South Orkney Islands (USA)

Arctic	Antarctic

Antarctic

1822–4 James Weddell reaches 74°15' in the Weddell Sea on the *Jane* and the *Beaufroy* (GB, Enderby)
1828–31 Henry Foster, on the *Chanticleer,* takes the first measurements of magnetism and gravity on Deception Island
1830–32 John Biscoe, on the *Tula* and the *Lively,* discovers Enderby Land, Adelaide Island, and Graham Land (GB, Enderby)
1837–40 Jules Dumont d'Urville, sailing on the *Astrolabe* and the *Zélée,* discovers Terre Adélie and the Clarie coast. He succeeds in determining the position of the South Magnetic Pole (France)
1838–9 John Balleny discovers the Balleny Islands on the *Eliza Scott* and the *Sabrina* (GB, Enderby)
1838–42 Charles Wilkes leads an expedition with the *Vincennes,* the *Peacock,* the *Porpoise,* the *Seagull,* the *Flying Fish,* and the *Relief.* Discovers Wilkes Land aboard the *Vincennes* and the *Peacock* (USA)
1839–43 James Clark Ross discovers Victoria Land, the Mount Erebus volcano and the Ross Ice Shelf on the *Erebus* and the *Terror.* Determines the position of the South Magnetic Pole (GB)

Arctic

1845–7 Sir John Franklin goes in search of the Northwest Passage in the *Erebus* and the *Terror* and loses his life in the attempt (GB)
1872–4 Karl Weyprecht and Julius Payer discover Franz Josef Land aboard the *Tegethof.*
1875–6 George Nares reaches 83°20'N on the *Alert* and the *Discovery* and explores the coast of Ellesmere Island (GB)
1879–81 De Long drifts in the Arctic Ocean on the *Jeannette* and is shipwrecked (USA)
1881–4 Greely winters at Fort Conger and beats Nares' record attempt on the Pole by 4 miles (USA)
1882–3 First International Polar Year
1888 Fridtjof Nansen crosses the Greenland inland ice sheet from east to west (Norway)
1891–1902 Peary explores north Greenland and Ellesmere Island; reaches 84°17'N in his first attempt to reach the Pole (USA)
1893–6 Nansen drifts on the *Fram* across the Arctic Ocean (Norway)
1894–7 Jackson winters in Franz Josef Land
1898–1902 Otto Sverdrup spends several winters on the coast of Ellesmere Island aboard the *Fram* and explores the west of the archipelago, claiming it for Norway (Norway)
1899–1900 The Duke of the Abruzzi winters on Rudolf Island; his second-in-command, Umberto Cagni, marginally beats Nansen's record in the quest for the North Pole (Italy)

1892–4 C. A. Larsen penetrates the Weddell Sea in the *Jason* and discovers the Larsen Ice Shelf (Norway)

1897–9 Adrien de Gerlache winters in the Bellingshausen Sea aboard the *Belgica* (Belgium)
1898–1900 Carstens Egeberg Borchgrevink, on the *Southern Cross,* establishes the first base on the continent at Cape Adare (GB)

1901–4 Robert F. Scott winters in McMurdo Sound with the *Discovery* (GB)
1901–3 Erich von Drygalski winters in Kaiser Wilhelm II Land with the *Gauss* (Germany)

Arctic	Antarctic
	1901–3 Otto Nordenskjöld sails on the *Antarctic* commanded by Larsen. Winters on Snow Hill Island. The *Antarctic* is crushed by ice, and Argentinians come to the rescue.
	1902–4 William Bruce discovers Coats Land in the Weddell Sea on the *Scotia* (GB)
1903–5 Roald Amundsen discovers the Northwest Passage aboard the *Gjoa* (Norway)	**1903–5** Jean-Baptiste Charcot sails to Booth Island on the *Français* and makes a hydrographic survey up to Alexander Island (France)
1905–6 Peary makes a new attempt on the Pole and reaches 87°06′N (USA)	
1906–8 Mylius Erichsen explores the northeast coast of Greenland and finds serious errors in Peary's maps (Denmark)	
1908–9 Peary announces that he reached the North Pole in April 1909 (USA)	**1907–9** Ernest Shackleton winters on Ross Island with the *Nimrod* and gets within 97 nautical miles of the Pole (GB)
Cook announces that he reached the North Pole in April 1908 (USA)	**1908–10** Charcot winters on Petermann Island with the *Pourquoi-Pas?* and carries on the work of his first expedition (France)
1909–12 Mikkelsen confirms this and extends Mylius Erichsen's discoveries in Greenland (Denmark)	**1910–2** Roald Amundsen winters at the Bay of Whales with the *Fram* and is first at the South Pole (Norway). Robert F. Scott winters on Ross Island with the *Terra Nova*, reaches the Pole, and dies with his four companions on the return (GB)
1912 Knud Rasmussen crosses north Greenland with 34 sleds and 353 dogs (Denmark)	**1911–2** Choku Shirase sails on the *Kainan Maru* aiming for the Pole. He explores King Edward VII Land (Japan). Wilhelm Filchner discovers the Filchner Ice Shelf at the end of the Weddell Sea aboard the *Deutschland* (Germany)
1913–5 Vilkitski makes the first east-west crossing of the Northeast Passage aboard the *Taymyr* and the *Vaygach* (Russia)	**1911–4** Douglas Mawson, aboard the *Aurora*, winters at Cape Denison on the Shackleton Ice Shelf and on Macquarie Island (Australia)
1913–7 Macmillan explores the far northwest of the Canadian archipelago. He shows that Crooker Land, discovered by Peary, does not exist (USA)	
1913–8 Stefansson explores the Beaufort Sea with the Canadian Arctic expedition aboard the *Karluk*	
1916–9 Rasmussen explores northwest Greenland; Thule II expedition (Denmark)	**1914–6** Ernest Shackleton sails on the *Endurance* and fails in his attempt to cross the Antarctic. The *Endurance* sinks, but Shackleton rescues all his men (GB)
1920–3 Lauge Koch makes an expedition on the bicentenary of Hans Egede's arrival in Greenland (Denmark)	**1921–2** Shackleton sails on the *Quest*; the expedition is curtailed after his death (GB)
1922–4 Amundsen drifts in the Arctic Ocean on board the *Maud* (Norway)	
1923–4 Rasmussen crosses the Northwest Passage on the Thule V expedition. He does ethnographic and archaeological research.	
1925 Amundsen flies to the North Pole with Lincoln Ellsworth (USA)	
1926 Richard E. Byrd announces he has reached the North Pole by air (USA)	
Amundsen, Ellsworth, and Umberto Nobile cross the Arctic Ocean from Spitsbergen to Alaska on the airship *Norge* (Norway, USA)	

Arctic	Antarctic
1928 Wilkins and Eielson fly from Alaska to Spitsbergen by airplane (Australia) Nobile reaches the North Pole in the airship *Italia*, which crashes on the return (Italy)	**1928–30** Hubert Wilkins makes the first Antarctic flight with two Lockheed Vega monoplanes (USA, GB) **1928–30** Richard Byrd winters at Little America, flies to the Pole with a three-engine Ford and two other planes, and discovers some mountains (USA) **1929–31** Douglas Mawson maps the coast between 75° and 45°E aboard the *Discovery* (Australia)
1930–2 Alfred Wegener makes an expedition to Greenland (Germany) **1930–2** George Alexavish Ushakov explores the whole northern archipelago (USSR) **1931** Watkins commands the British Arctic Air Route Expedition to Greenland; Courtault winters alone on the inland ice sheet for six months (GB). Wilkins makes a submarine Antarctic expedition in the *Nautilus* (Australia) **1932–3** Second International Polar Year	
	1933–5 Richard Byrd returns to the base of Little America and winters alone 125 miles to the south (USA) **1933–6** Lincoln Ellsworth makes the first transantarctic flight with a Northrop monoplane (USA) **1934–7** John Rymill winters with the British Graham Land Expedition and the *Penola* (GB)
1937–8 Ivan Papanin establishes the first drifting observatory at the North Pole (USSR)	**1938–9** Albert Ritscher sails on the *Schwabenland* and investigates the length of the Princess Martha coast in the summer (Germany)
1940 The German ship *Komet* crosses the Northeast Passage in two months to operate in the South Pacific (Germany)	**1939–41** Richard Byrd stays at the bases of Little America and Stonington Island (USA)
	1943–62 Falkland Islands Dependencies Survey. Numerous scientific projects and expeditions from bases established in Graham Land. FIDS replaced by British Antarctic Survey in 1967 (GB) **1946–7** Operation Highjump: commanded by Richard Byrd and Admiral Cruzen, 4000 men from the US Navy work on the aerial photography of the continent (USA) **1947–8** Finne Ronne winters at Marguerite Bay near the British base (USA) **1947–8** Operation Windmill, under Commander Ketchum, completes the work of Operation Highjump (USA) **1947–55** Annual expeditions of the Chilean government in the Antarctic peninsula (Chile) Argentine government active in Antarctic peninsula (Argentina)
1948 The Soviets organize annual aerial expeditions at high latitudes to establish research stations on the Arctic ice pack during the spring (USSR) **1948–53** Paul-Emile Victor organizes several expeditions and wintering parties in Greenland with the French Polar Expeditions (France)	**1949–52** John Giaever and Norwegian-Swedish-British expedition winter at Maudheim (International)

Arctic	Antarctic
	1949–53 André Liotard, Michel Barré, Mario Marret organize the first three winter seasons in Terre Adélie; the ships are the *Commandant-Charcot* and the *Tottan* (France)
1950–86 The Soviets establish 27 drifting stations on the lines of Papanin's to explore the Arctic Ocean and study its climate (USSR)	
1950–1 Jean Malaurie winters with the Thule Eskimos and makes an expedition to Inglefield Land (France)	
1952–4 Cortlandt J. W. Simpson and the British North Greenland Expedition in Queen Louise Land (GB)	
1952–60 The Americans establish a research station on a floe, T3, which drifts for eight years in the Arctic Ocean (USA)	**1954–5** Phillip Law, aboard the *Kista Dan,* establishes the first postwar Australian base (Australia)
	1955–8 Sir Vivian Fuchs, with the support of Sir Edmund Hillary, crosses the Antarctic (GB, NZ)
1958 The American submarine the *Nautilus* crosses the Arctic Ocean via the North Pole (USA)	**1957–8** From the start of the International Geophysical Year twelve countries, rising to eighteen, coordinate their research in some 50 stations and on overland and aerial expeditions over the inland ice sheet.
1959 The American submarine the *Skate* surfaces at the North Pole (USA)	
1959–74 International Glaciological Expedition to Greenland (5 countries)	
1962 The Soviet submarine the *Leninski Komsomolets* reaches the North Pole (USSR)	
1966 The Americans take ice samples 4500 feet deep at Cape Century, Greenland (USA)	**1967** The British Antarctic Survey is put under the umbrella of the Natural Environment Research Council (GB)
1968 Plaisted's expedition reaches the North Pole on a snowmobile on 20 April (USA)	**1968** The Americans drill 7100 feet at the base of Byrd, alone in reaching the rocky substratum (USA)
1968–9 Wally Herbert and the Transarctic Expedition go from Point Barrow to Spitsbergen with dogsleds (GB)	**1968–9** Japanese expedition from the base of Syowa to the South Pole and back, over 3700 miles (Japan)
1971 The British submarine the *Dreadnought* reaches the North Pole (GB)	
1977 The Soviet icebreaker the *Arktika* reaches the North Pole in August (USSR)	**1975–7** Claude Lorius directs Operation Dome C with aerial support from the Americans. He drills 2950 feet at an altitude of 10,500 feet (France)
1978 Naome Uemura makes a solo journey from Cape Columbia to the North Pole with a dogsled and 17 dogs (Japan)	
1979 D. I. Shparo and six companions reach the Pole after a march of 930 miles without dogs or sleds	**1979–82** Ranolph Fiennes makes a transglobal expedition across the Arctic and Antarctic
1983–4 Operation Mizex studies the influence of the Arctic Ocean on its surrounding countries (10 countries)	**1985–6** Roger Swan, Roger Mear, and Gareth Wood reach the South Pole in January 1986, following in the footsteps of Scott (GB)
1986 Will Steger and Jean-Louis Etienne independently reach the Pole in early May (US, France)	**1986–7** Monica Kristensen and Neil Macintyre make glaciological observations along the route taken by Amundsen (Norway, GB)
1988–91 GRIP (Greenland Ice Sheet Project) takes samples of ice at a depth of 11,200 feet in the center of Greenland (72°34'N and 37°37'W) (European Foundation of Science)	

Further Reading

Books

Amundsen, Roald, *The North West Passage*, repr. of 1980 ed., AMS Press, New York

————, *The South Pole*, trans. by A. G. Chater, Barnes and Noble, New York, 1976

Armstrong, Terence, *Russians in the Arctic*, Essential Books, Fair Lawn, New Jersey, 1958

————, *The Circumpolar North: A Political and Economic Geography of the Arctic and Sub-Arctic*, Methuen, London, 1978

Byrd, Richard E., *Alone*, repr. of 1938 ed., Island CA, Washington, D.C., 1984

————, *Discovery: The Story of the Second Byrd Antarctic Expedition*, repr. of 1935 ed., Ayer Co. Pubs., New York

Cook, Frederick, *Through the First Antarctic Night, 1898–1899*, McGill-Queens University Press, Montreal, 1980

Dufek, George, *Operation Deepfreeze*, Harcourt, Brace, and World, New York, 1957

Etienne, Jean-Louis, *Le Marcheur du Pôle*, R. Laffont, Paris 1986

Fogg, Gordon E., and David Smith, *The Explorations of*

Antarctica, Sterling, New York, 1990

Franklin, John, *Narrative of a Journey in the Shores of the Polar Sea in the Years 1819–1822*, repr. of 1823 ed., Greenwood Press, Westport, Connecticut

Fuchs, Vivian E., *Of Ice and Man*, Longwood Pub. Group, Wakefield, New Hampshire, 1984

Herbert, Wally, *Across the Top of the World: The Last Great Journey on Earth*, Putnam, New York, 1971

Kirwan, Laurence P., *A History of Polar Exploration*, Norton, New York, 1960

Lehane, Brendan, *The Northwest Passage*, Silver Burdett Press, Englewood Cliffs, New Jersey, 1982

Lopez, Barry, *Arctic Dreams*, Scribner, New York, 1986

Malaurie, Jean, *The Last Kings of Thule*, Dutton, New York, 1982

May, John, *The Greenpeace Book of Antarctica*, Doubleday, New York, 1960

Nansen, Fridtjof, *In Northern Mists: Arctic Exploration in Early Times*, repr. of 1911 ed., AMS Press, New York

————, *Norwegian North Pole Expedition in 1893–96: Scientific Results*, repr. of 1906 ed., Greenwood Press, Westport, Connecticut

Nordenskjöld, Nils A. E., *The Voyage of the Vega Round Asia and Europe*, repr. of 1882 ed., AMS Press, New York

Peary, Robert, *The North Pole*, F. A. Stokes, New York, 1910

Rasmussen, Knud, *Across Arctic America*, Greenwood Press, Westport Connecticut, 1969

Scott, Robert F., *Scott's Last Expedition: The Personal Journals of Captain R. F. Scott, R. N., C. V. O., on his Journey to the South Pole*, J. Murray, London, 1968

————, *The Voyage of the Discovery*, J. Murray, London, 1929

Shackleton, Ernest H., *The Heart of the Antarctic*, W. Heinemann, London, 1909

————, *South: The Story of Shackleton's Last Expedition*, W. Heinemann, London, 1970

Victor, Paul-Emile, *Man and the Conquest of the Poles*, Simon and Schuster, New York, 1958

Walton, David W. H., *Antarctic Science*,

Cambridge University Press, New York, 1987

Worsley, Frank, *Shackleton's Boat Journey*, Norton, New York, 1977

Periodicals

Antarctic Journal of the U.S., National Science Foundation, Washington, D.C.

Arctic, published by the Arctic Institute of North America, Calgary.

Arctic Research of the U.S., National Science Foundation, Washington, D.C.

Polar Record and *Polar and Glacier Abstracts*, published by the Scott Polar Research Institute, Cambridge, England.

Internord, published by the Centre d'Etudes Arctiques, Paris.

In addition, the *National Geographic* magazine of the National Geographic Society, Washington, D.C., regularly publishes illustrated accounts of expeditions.

Atlases

Polar Atlas, CIA, Washington D.C., 1980.

The Arctic and Antarctic Institute in St. Petersburg has published two magnificent atlases in Russian, one on the Arctic, the other on the Antarctic.

List of Illustrations

Museums

ENGLAND

Cambridge
Scott Polar Research
Institute

Records of British
expeditions, particu-
larly those of Franklin,
Scott, and Shackleton.

Greenwich
National Maritime
Museum

London
James Caird, the
whaler aboard which
Shackleton sailed to
South Georgia to
seek help.

NORWAY

Oslo
The *Fram* and
the *Gjoa* are kept
near Oslo and are
open to visitors.
Fridtjof Nansen's
house is also open
to the public.

SCOTLAND

Dundee
The *Discovery* is on
exhibit.

USSR

St. Petersburg
Arctic and Antarctic
Institute

Index

Photograph Credits

Andréemuseet, Granna 66a, 66b, 66–7. APN, Paris 28b, 114, 119, 162, 163, 165ar. Archiv für Kunst und Geschichte, Berlin 12. Aschehoug, Oslo 57, 63. BBC Hulton Picture Library, London 139, 164. Bibliothèque de l'Institut, Paris 26, 27. Bibl. Nat., Paris 14, 28–9. Bodleian Library, Oxford 18. Bridgeman Art Library, London 80–1, 88, front cover. British Antarctic Survey, Cambridge, England 125, 173. Bulloz, Paris 17b. Charmet, Paris 16, 30, 42, 69, 82–3, 85a, 85b, 86, 185. Dagli-Orti, Paris 22, 68. Edimages, Paris 36. E.T. Archives, London 1–9, 13, 21, 33, 99. Expéditions Polaires Françaises, Paris 112a, 120–1, 122–3. Explorer Archives, Paris 15, 24–5. Explorer/Lorius, Paris 161b. Glydendal, Oslo 72, 73. Robert Guillard, Paris 108, 112b, 169, 174. Wally Herbert 151. Jacana/Suinot, Paris 121b, 158a, 158b, 159b, 160l, 160r, 161a. Ash Johnson, British Antarctic Survey 173. Keystone, Paris 90a, 105. Roger Kirchner 121b. Claude Lorius, Grenoble 166. Mansell Collection, London 100. Musée MacCord, Montreal 50–5, back cover. NASA, Washington, D.C 109. National Maritime Museum, Greenwich, London 46, 48–9. Nationalmuseum, Stockholm 58. National Portrait Gallery, London 43. Navy Academy and Museum, Annapolis 39. Gertrude Nobile, Rome 75, 76–7, 77r. Giraudon, Paris 34. Old Dartmouth Historical Society, New Bedford Museum 128. Pitch/Paul-Emile Victor, Paris 111, 170, 181. P.P.P., Paris 106, 116–7. Rights Reserved 17a, 19, 23, 37, 47a, 59, 64–5, 87, 90b, 91, 101, 122a, 129, 130, 131, 132, 133, 135, 136, 137, 159a, 164, 178, 179b. Roger-Viollet, Paris 70, 184, spine. Royal Geographical Society, London 102, 104. Sipa-Press, Paris 127. Société de Géographie, Paris 35, 60, 61, 71. Scott Polar Research Institute, Cambridge, England 11, 31, 32, 40–1, 44, 45, 47b, 62, 78, 79, 89, 92a, 92–3, 94–5, 96–7, 102, 138, 140–6, 148–9, 154, 155, 157a, 157b, 179a. Stato Maggiore Aeronautica, Rome 74. Sygma/Préau, Paris 118. Wegener Institut, Bremenshaven 110, 165b.
Maps: Patrick Merienne, Paris 38, 56, 98, 113, 147, 176–7

Acknowledgments

The publishers thank the following people and institutions: Terence Armstrong, Cambridge University; (pp. 152–3) the Canadian Hydrographic Service, Ottawa, the International Hydrographic Bureau, Monaco, and the Intergovernmental Oceanographic Commission, UNESCO, Paris, for permission to reproduce GEBCO chart 517; (pp. 150–3) Editions du CNRS, Meudon, and Wally Herbert for permission to reproduce Wally Herbert's "The First Surface Crossing of the Arctic Ocean," *Pole Nord 1983*, 1987; Robert Guillard, explorer; Mr. Headland, Scott Polar Research Institute, Cambridge, England; Claude Lorius, Laboratoire de glaciologie de Grenoble; Jean Malaurie, Centre d'études arctiques, Paris; Gordon Robin, Cambridge University; Michel Roethel, bookseller, Ile Mysterieuse

Bertrand Imbert was an officer in the Free French navy.
In 1949 he took part in the first French expedition to
Terre Adélie and returned in 1950 with the Barré
expedition. In 1955 the Académie des Sciences put him
in charge of Antarctic expeditions during the
International Geophysical Year. He spent another winter
in Terre Adélie in 1957. Bertrand Imbert has published
numerous articles in polar and scientific journals.

Translation from the French by Alexandra Campbell

Project Manager: Sharon AvRutick
Typographic Designer: Elissa Ichiyasu
Design Assistant: Tricia McGillis
Editorial Assistant: Jennifer Stockman

Library of Congress Catalog Card Number: 91–75508

ISBN 0–8109–2881–7

Copyright © Gallimard 1987

English translation copyright © 1992 Harry N. Abrams, Inc., New York,
and Thames and Hudson Ltd., London

Published in 1992 by Harry N. Abrams, Incorporated, New York
A Times Mirror Company

Printed and bound in Italy by Editoriale Libraria, Trieste